OCTOBER, 1935
Downtown Gallery, New York

ARTHUR G. DOVE

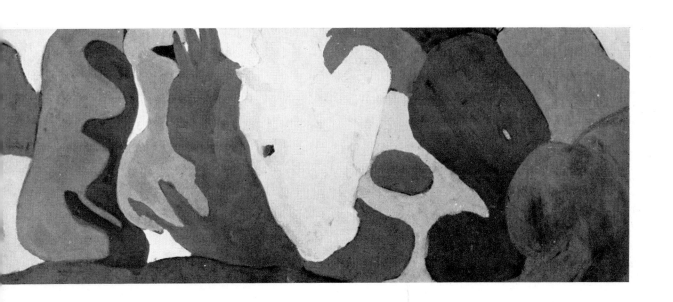

SAND BARGE, 1930
Phillips Gallery, Washington, D.C.

ARTHUR G.

BY FREDERICK S. WIGHT

UNIVERSITY OF CALIFORNIA PRESS
BERKELEY AND LOS ANGELES 1958

WILLOW TREE, 1938
Norton Gallery of Art, Palm Beach

University of California Press
Berkeley and Los Angeles, California

Cambridge University Press
London, England

© 1958, by The Regents of the University of California

Printed in the United States of America
by the University of California Printing Department

Library of Congress Catalog Card Number: 58–10625

Published for the Art Galleries, University of California, Los Angeles

Designed by Adrian Wilson

"I should like to enjoy life by choosing all its highest instances, to give back in my means of expression all that it gives to me, to give in form and color the reaction that plastic objects and sensations of light from within and without have reflected from my inner consciousness. Theories have been outgrown, the means is disappearing, the reality of the sensation alone remains. It is that in its essence which I wish to set down. It should be a delightful adventure."

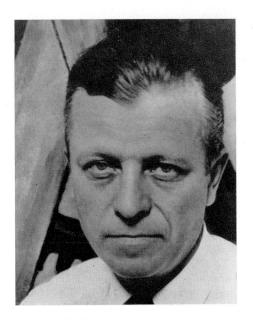

ARTHUR G. DOVE
Photograph by Alfred Stieglitz

TANKS, 1938
William H. Lane Foundation, Leominster, Massachusetts

ACKNOWLEDGMENTS

This book was published on the occasion of the Arthur G. Dove Retrospective Exhibition, organized by the Art Galleries of the University of California, Los Angeles, in association with the following institutions: Whitney Museum of American Art, New York; Phillips Gallery, Washington, D.C.; Museum of Fine Arts, Boston; Marion Koogler McNay Art Institute, San Antonio; Art Center in La Jolla; San Francisco Museum of Art.

Thanks are due to Georgia O'Keeffe and to the Alfred Stieglitz Archive, Yale Collection of American Literature, for permission to quote from the letters of Arthur G. Dove to Alfred Stieglitz, and to print Dove's *The Train Left Without Them;* to Suzanne Mullett Smith for her generous assistance and for the quotations from her thesis, "Arthur G. Dove," American University, Washington, D.C.; to Samuel M. Kootz for selections from a letter from Dove printed in *Modern American Painters;* to the heirs of James Rosenfeld for the quotations from *Port of New York;* for the quotations from the art critics of *The New Yorker* magazine.

Mrs. Arthur G. Dove and William Dove were most helpful, and their assistance and comment were gratefully received. Mrs. Edith Gregor Halpert has been of invaluable assistance in providing much of the documentation, and through her broad personal experience of the development of American art. The staff of the Downtown Gallery, particularly Mrs. Nathaly Chase Baum and John Marin, Jr., were indefatigable in their help.

Miss Susan Haverstick is especially thanked for her editorial assistance.

Many lenders to the Dove Retrospective Exhibition most generously provided color plates. Inter-Cultural Publications made available seven plates that originally illustrated Dr. Robert Goldwater's excellent article in *Perspectives USA* (Number 2); the Baltimore Museum of Art and the Whitney Museum of American Art made plates available; and Time, Inc., gave permission to reproduce in color ABSTRACTION No. 2. To all these thanks are gratefully offered.

Credit is extended for permission to reproduce photographs provided by the Art Institute of Chicago, the Metropolitan Museum of Art, the Museum of Modern Art, and the Philadelphia Museum of Art.

SQUARE ON THE POND, 1942
William H. Lane Foundation, Leominster, Massachusetts

CONTENTS

FLOUR MILL II, 1938
Phillips Gallery, Washington, D.C.

FOREWORD

Arthur G. Dove deserves to be ranked with the dissimilar Kandinsky among the earliest abstract expressionists. Certainly in the realm of uncompromising and impetuous exploration Dove was the boldest American pioneer. He was and is unique. The significant fact in his uneventful and important life is that after his twenty-seventh year he renounced a career as a successful illustrator to paint in ways unprecedented among his fellow countrymen and different from anything that had been done or was later to be done in Europe.

Profound was his conversion in his years of decision to the concept of the intimately symbolical image, to be abstracted from nature and from the most familiar objects, as a new language for painting. While he was seeking for abstract equivalents to the character of his immediate environment and his everyday experience, the trend of the abstractionists abroad was toward intellectual analysis and geometrical fragmentation. Dove on the other hand hoped to express his inner self with sensuous and lyrical pictographs. Ready to endure any hardship and to make any sacrifice to paint as he pleased he became a rebel against the preconception, still too prevalent in American art schools and formidable in 1907, that realistic representation is the only excuse for any artist. He was not less inclined, as his experiments matured in the 1920's, to dissent from the idioms and ideas of Fauvism, futurism, and cubism, which had developed into styles among the European leaders of abstract painting. Compelled to support his own creative experiments, he resolved to farm and live in rural solitude where living costs were low and he could be free from the distractions of the art world. The soil attracted him, seemed to call him home. The forms in nature were to be his dictionary. The spirit that emanates from material substance would be his goal. For his own personal reasons Dove became a hermit. It soon was evident to him that it was his destiny to be a lonely independent artist. He would compose, with the consistency of true conviction, in a playful caprice of colored and textured shapes.

He had found a new direction—and it is still a new direction. Abstract expressionism has now become a proliferation of popular roads for international travel. Some of these thoroughfares seem to have started from

Dove's trail-blazing. Dove however was no "action painter," no dynamic doodler. He took full advantage of both accidents and free associations, but his mind and hand were under conscious control. In his FLOUR MILL he was certainly a prophet of colorful calligraphy that is seemingly spontaneous, that describes a moment of light but displays brush strokes handsomely self-sufficient and exciting. And yet automatism has only a remote resemblance to his conceptual metamorphosis from nature's form. Dove was a nature poet who had a genuine love for the soil, the sky, and the seasons. He will be remembered as one of the few great individualists and genuine nature lovers among the many contemporary painters of abstraction. One reason Alfred Stieglitz persisted in his faithful sponsorship of Dove, in spite of the obstacles and discouragement he encountered in trying to make him understood a few years ahead of his time, was that he found in him a rugged quality deriving more from the patterns of the American Indian than from European studios.

Dove had something quite original and unique to say. He was not only unafraid of change but courageous enough to be different from the other moderns and too personal to adhere to any school. The most important truth about Dove is that he had complete integrity. His art and his life were one. The world could take him or leave him. His appeal would always be to those who had not lost their zest for play and for making things musical to the eye.

My own discovery of Dove about 1922 was important in my evolution as a critic and collector. At that time I still had the writer's attraction to painters whose special qualities could be interpreted and perhaps even re-created in words. Fascinated from the first glimpse by Dove's unique vision, I found that I was being drawn to an artist because his appeal was exclusively visual, because his whimsically imaginative images were inseparable from his resourceful craftsmanship. He was so unstandardized that in his own period and country he embarrassed the literary critics, and even the painters and teachers of painting who deal in theories and group movements. Dove talked about the "special conditions of light" which had inspired him. However he was no analyst and no realist of light. Some tones were light-reflecting, and some in contrast were light-absorbent. Mat surfaces could be rich and sensuous. Flat painting, as in the sunlit wall of his FLOUR MILL, could be vibrant. Magic could come from contour and from color and texture and retain the first joy of direct experience. There was the earthy, the elemental, to be savored in paint, and yet subtleties of modulated tone were not to be thought inconsistent with nature's organic forms and the happy accidents that nature provides for art in time, light, and weather.

The first two years of exhibiting had been for Dove a time of publicity and controversy. His work was shown in New York and Chicago and attracted more critical attention then than in his later and greater years. First

RAIN OR SNOW, 1943–1944
Phillips Gallery, Washington, D.C.

Cows in Pasture, 1935
Phillips Gallery, Washington, D.C.

were the earth-colored pastels fresh from his life on the farm. Then came the period of collages conceived with the conviction, which Dove shared with the witty and ingenious Kurt Schwitters, that anything can be material to the creative designer. Such insistence upon the object revealed to Dove his own purpose, to create an abstract imagery that would contain and convey at least something of his rural or water-front existence. His raw materials included not only pigments, canvas, and panels, but sails, sand, moss, weathered wood, rusted iron. He loved the animals of the pasture and the barn, the wild life of the fields and the air. In the Museum of Modern Art viewers stop in pleased surprise before Dove's GRANDMOTHER, a portrait achieved with a sample of her needlework, a page from her Bible, a flower and fern pressed within, and shingles from her old house. In the collage GOIN' FISHIN', among the objects arranged and enclosed in a box are sections of bamboo rod, a charred stump from an old tree, buttons for eyes, and a glimpse of blue denim overalls. In Paris at the Jeu de Paume in 1938 that collage spoke of Mark Twain rather than of Braque, Gris, or Picasso.

Dove expressed unashamed worship of sun and moon. He looked right into the glow of the morning sun or into the face of the full moon as it arose above the haunted hills. He was aware of the cycles of life and death in nature, of the tree trunk returning to the soil while the wind blows and new life begins. Even as he dared to be romantic in his abstractions, so also he was among the first to be humorous, sometimes even nonsensical, while never ceasing to be an enchanting painter. In COWS IN PASTURE, the somnolent curves and the absorbent tans and greens and browns are expressive of the subject in its very essence. Black and white and dun-colored cows are huddled in a pasture. Their hindquarters are settled comfortably in mossy, congenial turf. A bull calf has a sleepy eye and there is a bit of clover on his brain. The lazy contours suggest the slow and drowsy rumination. Cows, too, have their stream of consciousness.

When Dove became an invalid because of a chronic heart condition, he did not permit the inactivity and confinement to end his career as a painter. It did not interfere with his annual exhibition at An American Place. It gave him time to develop further, to adapt technical execution to profoundly personal conceptions. In the joyously executed canvases of his last years, he was truly the master of his fate and the conqueror of his infirmity. Success had come at last. He died at the moment when the return to favor of romanticism and the sudden popularity of total abstraction made his lone pioneering and his romantic patterning worthy of comparison with the life and the inspired designs of the great Ryder. Art in his time had become too collective, but Dove had remained a unique individual. A poet-painter he was, but he was also and essentially a sound twentieth-century American craftsman who loved a good job of painting for its own sake.

DUNCAN PHILLIPS
Phillips Gallery,
Washington, D.C.

ROOFTOPS, 1941
William H. Lane Foundation, Leominster, Massachusetts

ARTHUR G. DOVE

BY FREDERICK S. WIGHT

More than a generation ago, before the First World War, there was an enormous gap between the taste of the American public and the new art of the twentieth century. This gap was crossed, but emphatically not closed, by the famous Armory Show of 1913, a massive importation of European art that successively shocked New York, Chicago, and Boston. The show ranged through the nineteenth century, rediscovered Cézanne, van Gogh, and Gauguin. It went on to confront America with the work of the tumultuous Fauves and displayed the inventions of the cubists while the paint was still fresh. This demonstration, put on by the Association of American Painters and Sculptors, naturally included the American artists' relatively cautious defiances. To all intents a show by artists for artists, its major accomplishment was to point to a shift in allegiance, a change in the orientation of the American artists' foreign policy, from an Anglo-Saxon to a Latin tradition. The public was not prepared to understand, but at least the crowds came, whether to fume or to laugh. Misapprehension defended itself, and "modern art" became notorious.

If the scope, the mass attack, of the Armory Show opened an era, there were people who had traveled, looked, and reflected before 1913, who had been abroad and had come back the wiser. In particular, Alfred Stieglitz, the photographer and impresario, had established a New York gallery, an enclave of awareness in an attic room.

Stieglitz had gone to Germany as a young man in 1881, where he spent the better part of a decade studying photography, mostly in Berlin. On his final return to New York in 1890 he entered the photoengraving and printing business. He activated the Camera Club and founded *Camera Notes* in 1897, a publication that he edited until 1902, when he gave it up and published *Camera Work* and *Photo-Secession*. This latter title was drawn, doubtless, from the Berlin Secession, a group that broke away from the Union of Berlin Artists, and held its first exhibition in 1899.

Photo-Secession served likewise as a name for the gallery. At 291 Fifth Avenue, Stieglitz' appeal was not to the mass; rather a sense of unique privilege obtained, an opportunity to rise above the taste of the "people." As a showman, Stieglitz was the master of the narrow aperture.

Stieglitz is here encountered as a dealer, but it must be remembered that he was one of America's foremost artists, whether in his writings, his talk, or his work with the camera, in which he was early and great. His photographs were intense and revealing, and they expanded contact with visual reality. He had a pre-Freudian flair for the sensuous symbol and for the meaning of images. Paradoxically, his work was modest in scale and of a refined detachment. He had a marvelous vitality, a sure intuition, and was aware of those limits and barriers against which an artist struggles. He was at once a pioneer and a finished product.

As a dealer, inevitably Stieglitz interpreted his painters to a public that was more his than theirs, and their independence was presented as detachment. This was peculiarly true of the aloof Arthur Dove. How much Stieglitz brought him forward, how much he sequestered him—for he had an instinct for artificial scarcity—is not easy to determine. It is time to let Dove stand clear; yet the fact remains that to this day Dove must be approached by way of Stieglitz.

TEAM OF HORSES, 1911
Dr. Mary C. Holt, New York

NATURE SYMBOLIZED NO. 2, 1911
Alfred Stieglitz Coll.,
Art Institute of Chicago

Stieglitz, with his instinct to dramatize and develop more talents and arts than his own, soon branched out in his showings and became purveyor of the new to America, then of the new *in* America. Early in 1908—his gallery at 291 had been open for two years—he showed some sixty drawings by Rodin, which the sculptor and Edward Steichen had selected; and three months later, in April, he showed Matisse drawings, water colors, lithographs, and oils, bringing the painter up to date. He hung Toulouse-Lautrec lithographs in 1909, and in 1910 Cézanne's lithograph THE BATHERS became the "first Cézanne publicly shown anywhere in America." In 1911 Stieglitz "introduced" Picasso with a drawing, and in 1913 he capped the Armory Show with Picabia; he showed Brancusi and Braque in 1914.

Stieglitz, meanwhile, began to shift his interest to American artists. Hartley he showed in 1909, Marin and Maurer in 1910, and in that same year he presented a Forum Exhibition of seven Americans which included a newcomer, Arthur Dove. Two years later, in the last days of February, 1912, he presented the Arthur G. Dove First Exhibition Anywhere that contained a remarkable series of symbolic paintings. "A series of abstracts," Stieglitz said of them. "The pastels he had ground himself. . . . So the pictures went up, and of course they were over the heads of the people. . . . They were beautiful, they were not reminiscent of anyone else."

The Dove exhibition progressed from New York to Chicago. The dates of the New York showing were February 27 to March 12, 1912, and the Chicago show opened on March 14, an impossibly close scheduling which suggests that the New York show closed early to take advantage of the

Chicago opportunity, or perhaps Dove simply left for the west with a port-folio of pastels under his arm. He appeared with his exhibition to explain what it was about, being young and hoping to convert. His paintings had made no great impression on New York, but in Chicago they created much more disturbance. In the following year, when the Armory Show moved from New York to Chicago in turn, Dove was spoken of somewhat blas-phemously as its John the Baptist.

Many exhibitions later, when Dove's life was spent and Stieglitz was more than eighty, the artist-dealer relationship was still in force. By that time Stieglitz had long limited himself to American art, and the talents that he

ABSTRACTION No. 2, 1910
Downtown Gallery, New York

CONNECTICUT RIVER, 1911–1914
Mrs. Edith Gregor Halpert, New York

presented as his legacy to the future were Dove, John Marin, and Georgia O'Keeffe. Of these three, Dove was still the least known and appreciated, whether it was that he was the most abstract, the furthest ahead of his time, or simply that he had been physically the least present. He offered no help to legend or to the legend-maker. His art, although difficult, was basically sunlit, masculine, and outward-facing, and provided little of the enticement that stems from available personality. He was truly a detached man, and he was allowed to remain detached.

For many years Dove had to look to a single patron, Duncan Phillips, who loyally helped support him. His letters move and embarrass with his modest hopes, and other painters were perhaps his widest audience. Yet his work expressed the period, and his NATURE SYMBOLIZED, a generic title for his paintings of 1911, is prophetic of more achievements than his own. By right instinct and at an early date, he knew that the twentieth-century painter must communicate with symbols, and he struck an even balance between outer world and inner life.

Dove was born in Canandaigua, New York, on August 2, 1880, the son of William George Dove and his wife Elizabeth, who named him Arthur Garfield after the two Republican candidates of that year. William Dove was a bricklayer, then a brickmaker, finally a successful contractor who built without too much recourse to blueprints and plans. He constructed buildings at Hobart College in Geneva, where his son Arthur, who was later a student, reflected that his father had used a mortarboard hereabouts instead of wearing one. At Geneva William Dove stacked up dollars along with the bricks, and became County Clerk and Fire Chief. He was a man of energy and principle—it is recorded that he refused some excessive profit during the First World War.

After two years of Hobart College, William Dove sent his son on to Cornell and insisted on a year of law in the hope that the young man would become a lawyer. His incapacity to appreciate his son's gifts was built from the ground up; he was disappointed when Arthur turned illustrator, reconciled when he made money, and aghast when he saw his first one-man show. Arthur Dove was then in difficulty and he asked his father to help him with a hundred dollars a month. For once even Stieglitz failed to persuade. "No," said William Dove, "I won't do it. I won't encourage this madness." The money did not matter to William Dove, and Arthur always hoped that his father would take a different view of his achievements, believing naïvely to the time of his father's death in 1926, that some favorable article—for there were many by then—might work a change.

Dove in his childhood, however, was not stinted. From private school to high school—when he was pitcher for the team—and later in college, he was given all the material advantages. "For the first twelve years I was an only child and naturally spoiled in the way my family wished me to be. At the age of twelve I became a brother, and therefore gained twice as much freedom. I resigned from the church at the same age owing to a difficulty with the clergy over Robert Ingersoll [the professional atheist] having a right to his opinions whether we agree with them or not." Evidently there was something unyielding in the family temperament.

Long before Arthur took this step, the boy had found a friend in a neighbor named Newton Weatherly, a truck farmer interested in natural history, who cultivated a home-grown transcendentalism on the side. This "little bit of a man" admirably supplied some sympathy the boy lacked, knew not to overvalue his own time, and took young Arthur, aged five to nine, fishing and hunting. Weatherly at seventy "could hit a quail from the hip" and, still more remarkably, "could open a chestnut burr with his bare heel." He included oil painting among his noneconomic interests and gave his young friend scraps of canvas which he took home and stretched on frames that he had been able to miter after a fashion, nailing pieces of wood across the back. With such preparation, Arthur painted in oil. It is a pity not to know more of Weatherly, who seems to have found the water of Walden Pond in the Finger Lakes. Dove made much of him in recollection, feeling that he provided him with the wisdom to turn toward nature and live with her, when the human bent is to turn away.

Then of course there was a lady schoolteacher who gave him painting lessons; together they managed a flower piece, a duet that was primarily her performance. At Cornell, Dove painted water colors, produced one oil landscape, and drew from casts as "a soft way to earn college credit." His instructor here was Charles Wellington Furlong, who was also an illustrator and writer for magazines, and who seems to have encouraged Dove to live by his pencil. Dove ran off to New York and attended the Art Students League for five days, and after graduation he worked for an "advertising man" in New York for fifteen dollars a week. He was also making Conté crayon drawings, and he soon shifted over to illustrating for a living.

The influence of Furlong invites speculation. By coincidence, I knew Furlong in my boyhood, but by that time he was an explorer just back from Patagonia with tinted slides as evidence, ready to recoup by a season on the platform, in frock coat, pointing with a long wand that lit up on the end and made a momentary white place on the screen as he brought his adventures into focus. What remain in recollection are Furlong's heroic abilities. He threw a steer at the Pendleton Round-up, and he had the fortitude to hold his hands locked behind him while he fell on his face—preparation for more than one career. In this wiry restless little transcriber of the wilds there was something of Theodore Roosevelt the explorer and amateur naturalist, of the American-in-the-face-of-nature brought up to date by Lowell Thomas. Dove may have been liberated by this facile reporting, and it would take time for him to discover how different his own response to nature would be.

A year after Dove left college he married a girl from home. His father helped him during the early uncertain days, but he was soon independent and illustrating for *Harper's, Scribner's, Collier's,* the *Saturday Evening Post,* and the old *Life,* the humorous magazine of the period that fed an appetite for sketchy naturalistic anecdote. Dove is not famous for his illustrations, but his pencil was soon in demand and he drew with easy assurance. There was no technical difficulty, no awkwardness, and he provided an instinctive legible humor that editors could use. Humor, of a different sort to be sure, more akin to the wry wit of Paul Klee, carries over into his painting where it is not always recognized, so serious is serious art. But—discounting the large symbolic eyes that occasionally look back from his canvases—he seems to have had his fill of the human figure as an illustrator. At all times Dove had a sense of what was more or less important to him, and he was prepared to sacrifice one thing for another. This held true not only in his art but in his life.

Dove had been painting on the side, mostly in pastels, and he wished to go abroad. Between 1906 and 1907 he had made four thousand dollars, an achievement that mellowed his father, who again added to his bank account. So staked, Dove went to France for eighteen months. In Paris, he came to know a fellow American, Alfred Maurer, and they undertook to "simplify impressionism" together.

Maurer made a spectacular transition to "modern" painting, abandoning a successful realistic portraiture of the Chase or Henri free and loaded brush to follow in the blaze of Matisse. For Maurer, this change had been as immediate and emotion-charged as a revivalist conversion, and the impulse

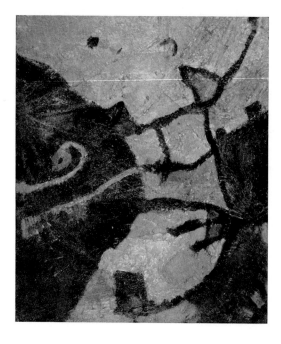

ABSTRACTION, 1914
Downtown Gallery, New York

PLANT FORMS, 1915
Gift of Mr. and Mrs. Roy R. Neuberger,
Whitney Museum of American Art, New York

behind the conversion was not far to seek. Maurer's father had been an illustrator for the popular print makers Currier and Ives, and he lived on doggedly to be a hundred, kept in existence, apparently, by his desire to triumph over his son. If the talented Alfred Maurer escaped into a new art and age where his father could not follow, some weakness or dependence, disguised as poverty, brought him back to physical degradation in his old home in New York. Here he survived miserably in a hall bedroom, his indomitable father on a stepladder watching through the transom to see what Alfie was painting now. At ninety-nine, Louis Maurer had a one-man show that won wide publicity both for its picturesque subject matter and the great age of the artist. He pushed on to the hundred mark, showed again, and then died, and his no-longer-young son committed suicide. This is not a digression, for Dove, by contrast, knew how to escape when illustration pursued, and he maintained a lifelong friendship with the lovable, gifted, and ailing Alfie.

In Paris, Dove also knew the sculptor Jo Davidson and the still-unappreciated American painter Arthur Carles.

All his life Dove needed the country. He stayed only briefly in Paris and

went south to Cagnes. The landscapes that he produced here gained from his knowledge of Cézanne. He was already something of an impressionist before he left America, but now, like the Fauves, he preserved the impressionist light even as he let a masonry of pigment stand clear. In France he exhibited twice in the Autumn Salon, in 1908 and by invitation in the following year. "American work wins high favor in Autumn Salon," was the heading of a column in the *New York World* of October 2, 1909, and the article concluded: "Arthur Dove, the New York illustrator, has a still life of conspicuous merit." This still life was THE LOBSTER (1908).

"Then back to America [wrote Dove] and discovered that at that time it was not possible to live by art alone." But to live by Stieglitz was another matter. "One fine day," said Stieglitz, "a man called Dove brought some of his work. I had shown Maurer and Marin. Dove and Maurer were intimates. Maurer was still in Paris. He wanted me to see Dove's work. Dove told me the story of his life." The "fine day" was late in 1909 or early in the next year, and Dove wrote of the place he found: "It was a place where anything could happen. A remarkable place. People, paintings, photographs, and writings, all working in a laboratory." When Stieglitz exhibited Dove's canvases in a group show, Younger American Painters, in March, 1910, THE LOBSTER drew the attention of the *New York World*. "Do you want your optic nerves stimulated so that you will see life with a new vision? Go and see Dove's delineation of a diabolical lobster who died a horrible death. Arthur Dove has done other things, but of all the paintings by him that are on view, no one [sic] shows so much feeling as that lobster. One would judge that it was painted from memory. . . . " The memory perhaps was of Cézanne for the painting was not yet Dove. It must not be forgotten that both Marin and Dove became themselves only after they met Stieglitz. Everything that went before was at once freed and formalized for Marin, freed and symbolized for Dove.

Elizabeth Luther Carey, in the *New York Times*, found THE LOBSTER "one of the most convincing canvases; but we confess ignorance of the general aim of the group, unless it is to make color and pattern do the work of a picture, leaving out values of dark and light, and substituting symbol for representation." This is not ignorance, but perception. A series of six abstractions, painted in 1910, show the artist freeing himself from the image or source, making quite clear that he is not distorting so much as substituting, and when this corner has been turned, progress is rapid. Between 1910 and 1912 he is creating paintings in pastel which are abstract and deliberate with the maturity of realized purpose. These paintings were at once recognized as new, whether they were accepted or not. Ten were shown in the Arthur G. Dove First Exhibition Anywhere, and Dove gave them the generic title THE TEN COMMANDMENTS.

The paintings in the exhibition presented a before-and-after appearance. The earlier paintings brought back from France were impressionist or postimpressionist, gay and blond; the new pastels were somber. It was THE TEN COMMANDMENTS that drew comment. Said the *Times,* March 3: "They are just plain pictures that mean nothing at all except that a certain combination of shapes and colors please the artist. . . . We have heard many an artist say that his work meant nothing but this, but we are seldom so completely convinced as by Mr. Dove's untitled pictures. . . . If it gives pleasure to the eye to see rich sunsets and greens and silvery blues brought together in irregular geometrical segments, the owner of the fortunate eye will like the exhibition; otherwise not."

The *Evening Mail,* March 21, under "Pattern Paintings by A. G. Dove," conveniently helps identify the pastels: "Mr. Dove paints in patterns, but he does not scorn to borrow his patterns from nature. This picture consists in a design of a boat's sails; that one, of steep roofs seen through a window; that one, of the fronds of lilies, or agaves; and so on. . . . Here is a strange picture that seems to have, at the right, a large blue comma; and then some upward pointed horns of light blue, dark blue, and other colors. What is it all about? No one can tell—and yet the result is strangely agreeable." And a week later, March 9, in the same paper, Mr. Chamberlain found "an extraordinary fascination about some of these decorative squares that he calls paintings. In color they are beautiful and strange, and the eye returns to them again and again as if with delight at finding something which it is not required to understand at all, but which is intrinsically agreeable."

Dove himself commented on THE TEN COMMANDMENTS in a letter to Samuel Kootz: "Then one day I made a drawing of a hillside. The wind was blowing. I chose three forms from the planes on the side of the trees, and three colors, and black and white. From these was made a rhythmic painting that expressed the spirit of the whole thing. The colors were chosen to express the substance of these objects and the sky. These colors were made into pastels, carefully weighed out, and graded with black and white into an instrument to be used in making that certain painting. There were nine others, each with its own different motive. I took them to Stieglitz. He made room for them in 1912."

When the show went to Chicago, Dove stayed at the old Auditorium hotel, housed, as it thus happened, by the then living and drinking Louis Sullivan. Dove was confident and even wrote Marin to come out to try his luck. The exhibition, at the W. Scott Thurber Galleries, offered a subheading to prepare the public: "The paintings are examples of that new thought in modern art known as the Matisse movement, Post Impressionism, or the more defining term of Expressionism." Dove was on hand to unravel this statement. "Now comes Arthur Dove himself," says the *Record-Herald*, March 19, "a modest young man with theories, also with an exhibition. On one side of the room he has his discarded conservative manner of the post-impressionist fraternity. These examples he tolerates merely as records along a path of evolution. It might be added that some of them are very tender in their suggestions of moods." The reviewer then turns his back on the paintings from Cagnes. "Opposite these are the real Dove creations, the radicals of radicals. These present no attempt at representation of form but of the abstract idea of form . . . or of some . . . sensation or emotion. They delineate, in other words, a series of symbols. . . ."

The *Chicago Examiner*'s society column quotes Dove: "I don't like titles for these pictures, because they should tell their own story. You can see that forms repeat themselves in various phases of light, and that convolutions of form are the results of reflections in nature. Yes, I could paint a cyclone. . . . I would show repetitions and convolutions of the rage of the tempest. I would paint the wind, not a landscape chastized by the cyclone." Harriet Monroe, in the *Chicago Tribune*, March 17, also had been listening: "Modern minds, he thinks, are reaching out toward an art of pure color and form dissociated from 'representation.'"

Then toward the end of the exhibition, Bert Leston Taylor put Dove into verse in the *Chicago Tribune*, March 27. His jingle had survival power and was several times reprinted, finally in *Collier's*.

Written after viewing Mr. Dove's exhibition of the

"SIMULTANEOUSNESS OF THE AMBIENT"

I cannot tell you how I love
The canvases of Mr. Dove,
Which Saturday I went to see
In Mr. Thurber's Gallery.

At first you fancy they are built
As patterns for a crazy quilt
But soon you see that they express
An ambient simultaneousness.

This thing, which you would almost bet
Portrays a Spanish omelette,
Depicts instead, with wondrous skill,
A horse and cart upon a hill.

Now Mr. Dove has too much art
To show the horse or show the cart;
Instead he paints the creak and strain
Get it? No pike is half so plain.

This thing, which would appear to show
A fancy vest scenario,
Is really quite another thing—
A flock of pigeons on the wing.

But Mr. Dove is much too keen
To let a single bird be seen;
To show the pigeons would not do
And so he simply paints the coo.

It's all as simple as can be;
He paints the things you cannot see,
Just as composers please the ear
With "program" things you cannot hear.

Dove is the cleverest of chaps;
And, gazing at his rhythmic maps,
I wondered (and I'm wondering yet)
Whether he did them on a bet.

Two days later George Cram Cook came out with a "causerie" in the *Chicago Evening Post Literary Review,* taking note of Mr. Taylor's poetry and playfully returning the subject to the seriousness it deserved. The causerie contains extraordinary comment:

Someone in every group quotes, "He paints the coo." How grateful they must be to B. L. T., being relieved by the phrase of the necessity of thinking.

—And the ten of these [COMMANDMENTS are] altogether much more interesting than any one of them singly. They show successive steps in his . . .

—In his groping.

—Groping is the word, all right. It's what les fauves are doing in Paris, in London, in America. And their work is the point of the wedge that is being driven into the future. This is the real creative art impulse of our century.

—That's the word—the self-significance of color and line—regardless of what the colors and lines represent, or whether they represent anything.

—In other words, this is presentative painting, not representative painting.

—Look out or you'll invent the name destined to replace the unmeaning term post-impressionism. Presentative painting—the presentativists.

—We can call the other study of circle and right angle presentative in spite of its suggestion of roofs and factory chimneys. It is the cutting, vertical lines of the chimneys—their cuttingness, their verticalness, their parallelness that interested the artist, not their chimneyness. He leaves chimneyness to photography. . . .

—Those two studies, whose thematic form works like a comma, are also purely presentative—the form Mr. Dove's interpreter said was a wind pattern. Absurd and unthinkable as a representation of wind, the canvas presents a linear theme in such a way as to make the eye follow the same kind of curve over and over again.

—That suggests a factor we hadn't thought of in the effect of this rhythmic presentation of line. As the eye follows these lines—the three sails, for instance, in the design of the sails, the muscles of the eye perform the same movement over and over. What's the psychological effect of that?

—What I would like to get hold of is the relation of this new painting to geometry and to music. We've mentioned the two circle-and-right-angle studies. There's also the cone-and-polygon picture which projects its theme into the cone of a steeple and the polygon of a tree outline behind the steeple.

—All of which will look perfectly absurd to anyone who cannot escape from his lifelong habit of comparing the elements of a painting not with each other but with his memory of represented objects.

—Escape from lifelong habit is just the liberation offered by art. That's why new art is necessary when old art has become fixed in habit.

—But tell me: is this new painting really trying, as some say, to be music, or is it painting trying to be more itself?

—I should say it was painting trying to use its own elements—lines, masses, colors—with the same freedom from representativeness which exists in musical notes—and rhythms. . . .

—The first time I went to see Dove's things I heard an art critic explaining that they and their kind were the degringolade—decadent, the work of men born too tired to carry on the old tradition of painting.

—They weren't born too tired. It was the old tradition—its present impoverishment—which made them tired. It's exhausted, not they. Anyone with eyes can see the new energy working here—breaking a way into the untried, experimenting, taking new hold of visual elements.

To examine THE TEN COMMANDMENTS as a group today requires an effort of reconstruction. But the effort is necessary if we are to see what art owes to Dove—the deliberateness with which he opened the door to abstraction before 1912. "THE TEN COMMANDMENTS were more intriguing than any one of them singly," wrote Cook. There is in existence a file checked over by Dove toward the end of his life which contains one tantalizing card for THE TEN COMMANDMENTS, simply giving their size as 18 × 23. Not surprisingly they were all of a size (vertical or horizontal, and within fractions of an inch), for they were treated as a distinct group both by the painter and by those who first saw them.

In the file checked over by Dove—and he was more meticulous in his records than Stieglitz, who tended to date paintings from the time of their ex-

SAILS, 1911
*Philip L. Goodwin Coll.,
New York*

33

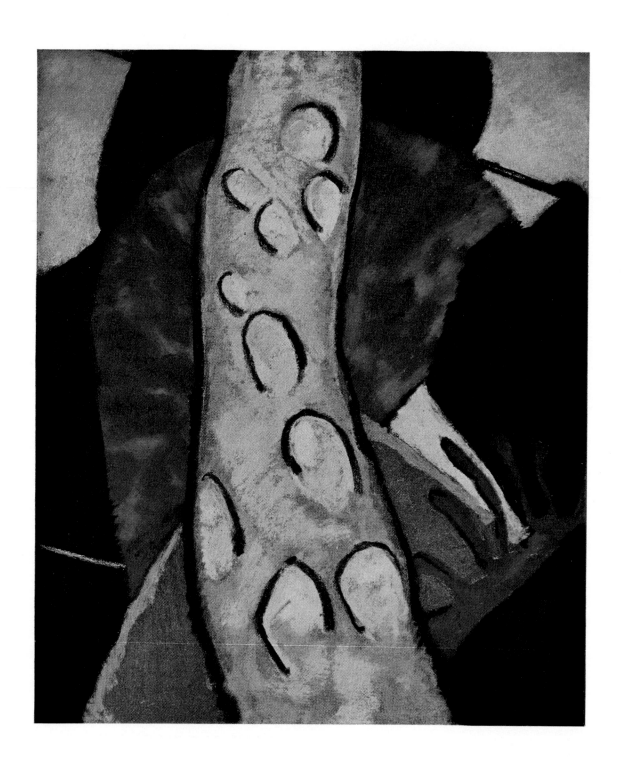

Awalk Poplars, 1920
Mrs. Edith Gregor Halpert, New York

hibition and changed names as he chose—the card, HORSE AND CART (1911 or 1912), has endorsed upon it, "Picture about which Bert Lester wrote." This work is of course identical with TEAM OF HORSES (1912), pastel 18½ × 21½, No. 9 in the catalogue of the White Art Museum Exhibition at Cornell, 1954; and Alan Solomon, in his essay in that catalogue, places this painting in the 1912 exhibition. WIND ON HILLSIDE (1911) was reproduced in the *Ladies Home Journal,* January, 1924, to illustrate an article, "The Crime Wave in Art," by Oliver Herford. Dove, goaded to comment, identified it as one of the series. Indeed, in his letter to Samuel Kootz in which he enlarges on his method, he seems to regard it as the key painting. Then there is SAILS (1911), which fits the references in the reviews of the New York and Chicago shows, and BASED ON LEAF FORMS AND SPACES reproduced in *Cubists, Post-Impressionists,* published by Arthur Jerome Eddy in Chicago in 1913. Identification rests on rock-solid ground here, as Eddy bought the painting out of the show (for fifty dollars, although it was marked one hundred and fifty) and had an exchange of letters with Dove in preparation for his text. Eddy later sold the painting to the British Consul in Chicago, and it was last seen in Warsaw. It is also certain that the exhibition contained COW (1911), the first of a long series.

MOVEMENT NO. 1 (1911?), of the Ferdinand Howell collection at the Columbus Gallery of Fine Arts, merits inclusion. But now caution is in order. WIND ON HILLSIDE, for instance, is also called NATURE SYMBOLIZED NO. 2 in the file referred to above, and in the same file FACTORY CHIMNEYS is NATURE SYMBOLIZED NO. 1. On the assumption that No. 1 is as early as No. 2, FACTORY CHIMNEYS is the painting described by Cook. FACTORY CHIMNEYS, however, bears the date 1914, and may well be a repeat of a composition that appeared two or three years earlier. We must content ourselves for the nonce with the thought that it is probably close enough to one of THE TEN COMMANDMENTS to extend our experience of the group. This also holds for CONNECTICUT RIVER (1914), which may be earlier than its given date, or may be a repeat. CONNECTICUT RIVER is of peculiar interest since it is recognizably a development of one of a group of six earlier oil studies that are quite abstract, all 9 × 10, and dated 1910 in the card file that Dove reviewed. It is impossible to imagine these little oils to be later than the mature pastels of the 1912 exhibition; in their handling, in the early maneuvering in thick paint, they are nearer to the canvases brought home from France. But it is also difficult to see four years between them and the CONNECTICUT RIVER which grows out of them. In short, the 1914 date of CONNECTICUT RIVER may not be early enough.

Finally, the very title, THE TEN COMMANDMENTS, is elusive. By 1916 Stieglitz was showing a whole group of undated Doves monotonously titled NATURE SYMBOLIZED. To find some of THE TEN COMMANDMENTS carded as NATURE SYMBOLIZED raises the suspicion that this latter title was devised and preferred by Stieglitz. NATURE SYMBOLIZED was not only more explanatory, but it did not limit the group to ten.

Other elusive paintings listed in the Dove file might be candidates for the group: CALF—ABSTRACT BIRTH OF A CALF (1911); PAGAN PHILOSOPHY (1910–1913), pastel, blue and brown, Stieglitz Collection; ROOFS (1910). But where is the painting containing the flight of pigeons, of which Dove only painted the coo?

By the time the show was over, Chicago had made a successful effort to understand, and even the rhyming Mr. Taylor seemed to get the point. The amount of ink spilled over Dove in Chicago is only indicated here. But sales were not proportionate. Even a would-be purchaser of THE LOBSTER retreated when Dove admitted that his new sober pastels interested him more. They indicated his future direction.

A friend, the actor William S. Hart, outlaw and sheriff of the silent films, advanced him the carfare back to New York.

When a man retreats from the world, his thoughts and concepts expand in self-imposed exile, and his solitude affords him the opportunity to speak to himself. Dove, however, reflected and then withdrew. He did not find thoughts in the wilderness, he took them there. He had a certain precocity, which he later disclaimed, and his ideas and theories developed early, as did his work, and changed remarkably little. They merely rounded themselves out. As he disengaged himself, he pared down his philosophy to conceptions that would serve; an economical man, he limited himself to practical essentials. His thoughts give meaning to the living-out of his life.

Arthur Jerome Eddy, who had purchased BASED ON LEAF FORMS AND SPACES out of the Chicago show, wrote to Dove and received an illuminating reply:

> My dear Mr. Eddy:
>
> You have asked me to "explain as I would talk to any intelligent friend, the idea behind the picture," or in other words, "what I am driving at."
>
> First of all this is not propaganda, there has been too much of that written on Modern Art already. It is simply an explanation of *my own means* in answer to the above question.
>
> In as much as the means continually changes as one learns, perhaps the best way to make it understood would be to state the different steps which have been taken up to the present time. After having come to the conclusion that there were a few principles existent in all good art from the earliest examples we have, through the masters to the present, I get about it to analyze these principles as they occurred in works of art and in nature.
>
> One of these principles which seemed the most evident was the choice of the simple motif. This same law held in nature, a few forms and a few

colors sufficed for the creation of an object. Consequently I gave up my more disorderly methods (impressionism). In other words I gave up trying to express an idea by stating innumerable little facts, the statement of facts having no more to do with the art of painting than statistics with literature. . . .

The first step was to choose from nature a motif in color and with that motif to paint from nature, the forms still being objective.

The second step was to apply this same principle to form, the actual dependence upon the object (representation) disappearing, and the means of expression becoming purely subjective. After working for some time in this way, I no longer observed in the old way, and, not only began to think subjectively but also to remember certain sensations purely through their form and color, that is, by certain shapes, planes of light, or character lines determined by the meeting of such planes.

With the introduction of the line motif the expression grew more plastic and the struggle with the means became less evident.

Dove was to remain conscious of lines and edges. For him, line was not in contrast to form and mass, it was a perimeter. If it moved, a mass behind it had life. The line-delimited forms, when they drew away from realism, either were swollen and flowing, pregnant forms, or they were pronged and sickle-shaped, cog forms, the teeth of a circular saw. Both are dynamic: the first sweeps and expands; the second cuts and tears.

Hutchins Hapgood, writing in the *New York Globe* in 1913, related that Dove walked into 291 and told Stieglitz that he had found his line had gone dead. " 'I thought,' he said, 'I could rely on my memory and on my warmth of vision and temperament alone to make my line live. But I find I cannot do it, and must return to a certain extent, but a certain extent only, to objective things or elements. I must make my line vital!'

"He must give up his intellectualism and get back to the simple feeling for life. He must feel the 'live line,' which stimulates life in the observer, which enhances existence, which is the essence of art, of morality, of love."

This language of course is the essence of Stieglitz; if traces of Dove appear in the first paragraph, Stieglitz is undiluted in the second. It is true, however, that Dove drew back at this time, or drew closer to nature in all humility in his life as well as in his works. The forms that he discovered were less brittle and arbitrary and more enveloping and healing, and he regarded the transformation of object into symbol as the golden mean between the arrogance of pure construction and the slavery of pure resemblance. In Dove's painting nature is like the pattern in polished marble: the pattern is altogether natural, yet not to be found until man has cut a plane through the rock.

In 1927 Dove wrote for a Stieglitz catalogue, "I should like to take wind and water and sand as a motif and work with them but it has to be simplified in most cases to color and force lines and substances, just as music has done with sound." "Force lines" is the most important phrase, and Alan Solomon in his essay for the Dove Retrospective Exhibition at Cornell says that it comes directly from the futurist vocabulary.

A phrase more of Dove's own is "condition of light." It appears in a letter printed three years later in Samuel Kootz's *Modern American Painters:*

> Then there was the search for a means of expression which did not depend upon representation. It should have order, size, intensity, spirit, nearer to the music of the eye.
>
> If one could paint the part that goes to make the spirit of painting and leave out all that just makes tons and tons of art.
>
> There was a long period of searching for a something in color which I then called "a condition of light." It applied to all objects in nature, flowers, trees, people, apples, cows. These all have their certain condition of light, which establishes them to the eye, to each other, and to the understanding.

SUMMER, 1935
William H. Lane Foundation, Leominster, Massachusetts

PIECES OF RED, GREEN & BLUE, 1944
William H. Lane Foundation, Leominster, Massachusetts

To understand that clearly go to nature, or to the Museum of Natural History and see the butterflies. Each has its own orange, blue, black; white, yellow, brown, green, and black, all carefully chosen to fit the character of the life going on in that individual entity.

After painting objects with those color motives for some time, I began to feel the same idea existing in form. . . .

This choice of form motives of course took the paintings away from representation in the ordinary sense.

On the one hand, Dove wanted the subjective response to an object, the color or form which the beholder assigned it; but on the other, this response must prove to be the quintessence of the thing, to be "true." The special quality that hovers over an object and provides its particularity is its "condition of light." For Dove, color and form symbolize the philosophic intangible beneath appearances; "condition of light" somehow describes an object's visual karma and becomes the guardian of its changeless personality.

In his effort to draw the special quality out of a particular color, he would set up a palette of black, white, and a single hue. One color, he taught his son, made colors out of black and white, and he would base his color compositions on various "triads." And the triangle on his palette somehow transformed the differences in color into direction; in the up-and-over "force lines" met.

He pulled up a cyclamen and tore it to pieces to show his son how the color went down into the stem and on into the root, how the color was all-pervasive, the flower's "condition."

"You can describe a person in a color."

"There is no such thing as abstraction."

"Everything we do is a self-portrait."

"Nothing has the speed of a line."

"I made a living farming and illustrating to support painting." Dove gave up a life of urban bohemian satisfaction at a time when painting and illustrating, creative writing and uncreative printing, were pleasantly confused in a genial freemasonry of their own. Dove used to frequent Mouquin's restaurant (the scene has been preserved if not immortalized by Glackens' painting) and here were Lawson, Sloan, Henri, and the burly Luks, unsqueamish painters to be known later as the Ash Can School. Other places to find Dove were the Café Francis, or Petit Pas, frequented by the painter William Yeats, remembered not for his paintings, but for having two sons who caught better the family tide of genius. Henri, too, would be here, the dean of the radicals, remembering Manet's once new ways. A dinner with wine cost fifty cents. It was not Paris, but it was liberty.

Dove and a fellow illustrator on *Life* began going to the San Carlos Café. Here Glackens joined them, and so did illustrators for the *New York Journal* and a political cartoonist for the *Evening World*, Clive Weed—perhaps incautiously, for he was married to a painter from Philadelphia, Helen Torr, who was to become Dove's second wife. At home among the journalist-illustrator gastronomists, Dove also had his place in the more distinguished group around Stieglitz, which included, at one time or another, Waldo Frank, Sherwood Anderson and Lachaise, Alfie Maurer and Georgia O'Keeffe. Maurer from a distance had first brought Dove into contact with Stieglitz; Dove in turn introduced Maurer to Sherwood Anderson, who bought and praised Maurer when purchase and praise were gravely needed. All this has an agreeable sound, and Dove described himself during these days as neither social nor unsocial. He was humorous, mellow rather than sharp, with a soft voice— "you had a hard time hearing him"—and his expression was open and direct.

He liked a party. He drank as he talked, when there was something to drink about. In his later more open-air days, when he rose at three-thirty to four in summer and six in winter and was in bed by nine, he would drink before lunch. He must be judged by his own timetable—noon for him was another man's five o'clock. In New York he was a joiner, on the members' committee of the Illustrators' Society, in the Players' Club, and to be seen on the fringe of the parties of the Publishers' Association. Yet he hated New York.

The time came when Dove was no longer comfortable thinking of himself as an illustrator. He wished to go back to the country, live in the open, and work and paint. In 1910, the year his son William Dove was born, he moved to Westport, Connecticut, and bought a farm. Two years later he bought another, half rock and half swamp, which seemed to him suitable only for raising chickens. "All of my young chicks come out of their eggs like pop-corn, almost seven hundred of them this year." If raising chickens was his goal, he succeeded. He fished for crabs, ground them up, and fed them to his flock. The crab shells became egg shells, and he was eventually accorded a prize by the Farm Board of the State of Connecticut. Working from 4 A.M. until midnight he managed to clear a hundred dollars a month, the sum he had set and his father had refused, as the price of a painter's independence.

But the hundred dollars a month were not enough and the hours were too long. Men who live on a poor soil near the sea take to the water, so Dove decided to become a lobsterman. He had a twelve-foot boat named the *Doughnut,* complete with engine and cabin, and his neighbors were Con-necticut lobstermen. This new venture, however, was brief enough. His neighbors liked him as a companion, but not as another lobsterman. In those days, rival fishermen on the Connecticut and Long Island shores used to cross the Sound at night and cut back and forth through the leaders of the fishtraps on the further side, a propeller proving an adequate weapon. Dove's neighbors were milder; they simply planted short lobsters in his lobster car and tipped off the game warden. Justice took its course, and Dove paid his fine and went back to illustrating for a while. But there was never any hard feeling on the part of his longshore friends.

During the early Westport years Dove experimented. A large ADAM AND EVE was overpainted indefinitely. He would work on it for a while to warm up before beginning something else. He said that he was "practicing scales." Of the little he produced in those years much was destroyed, enough to re-quire a ritual, devised by an etcher-lithographer friend; together they dug a hole behind the studio and buried the experiments. What remained, the Westport yield, was a modest number of pestels. His son was forbidden to go into the room where they were made, and he remembers that his father was rarely there.

Yet Dove was always in communication with Stieglitz. The two men wrote each other, Stieglitz preserving Dove's letters, which were the painter's mental lifeline, and Dove supplying with genuine dignity the devotion that

WATERFALL, 1925
Phillips Gallery, Washington, D.C.

was perhaps too much of a requisite, pouring it out over the years. In 1914 Stieglitz asked his artists to write their impression of 291, and Dove complied:

> My dear Stieglitz:
>
> I have been trying to answer your question ever since your letter came but found it rather difficult to express satisfactorily my ideas. Your request that as little reference be made to yourself as possible makes it doubly difficult. One might almost say that Stieglitz is 291. . . .
>
> The question "What is 291?" leaves one in the same position in explaining it as the modern painter is in explaining his painting. The modern painting does not represent any definite object. Neither does "291" represent any definite movement in one direction. Such as, Socialism, suffrage, etc. Perhaps it is these movements having but one direction that make life at present so stuffy and full of discontent.
>
> There could be no "291 ism." "291" takes a step further and stands for orderly movement in all directions. In other words it is what the observer sees in it—an idea to the (nth) power.
>
> One *means* used at "291" has been a process of elimination of the non-essential. This happens to be one of the important principles in modern art; there "291" is interested in modern art.
>
> It was not created to promote modern art, photography, nor modern literature. That would be a business and "291" is not a shop.
>
> It is not an organization that one may join. One either belongs or does not.
>
> It has grown and outgrown in order to grow. It grew because there was a need for such a place, yet it is not a place.
>
> Not being a movement, it moves. So do "race horses," and some people, and "there are all sorts of sports," but no betting. It is more interesting to find than to win.
>
> This seems to be "291" or, is it Stieglitz?
>
> This is as little reference to you as I can seem to make.
>
> With best wishes for the whole year.
>
> As ever
> Arthur G. Dove

In 1916 Stieglitz organized another Forum Exhibition, this time at the Anderson Galleries farther uptown. The sixteen Dove paintings were all titled NATURE SYMBOLIZED, and this very fact, added to Dove's known difficulties in production, suggests that the showing was something of a recapitulation. Charles Caffin covered the exhibition in the *New York American*:

> Dove calls his pictures "Nature Symbolized." Some are flat patterns, others go far back into space, but without a pronounced feeling for spatial structure. Their chief beauty is color, with its variety of expressional suggestion. And the latter is markedly personal; so personal, in fact to the artist that the impression produced in the spectator is in the first instance one of pleasurable sensation. But the impression deepens . . . the mental orderliness . . . the emotional and imaginative scope of Dove's work . . . express a conviction . . . the more one studies the work, the more it penetrates one's consciousness.

Cow I, 1935
*Randolph-Macon
Woman's College,
Lynchburg, Virginia*

As if to defend himself against words, Dove condensed a life into a sentence for the 1916 catalogue:

> My wish is to work so unassailably that one could let one's worst instincts go unanalyzed, not to revolutionize nor reform but to enjoy life out loud . . . that is what I need and indicates my direction.

The days at 291 were running out. Stieglitz the pioneer had a way of exhausting a situation, like a plot of ground, then moving on and rebeginning. He closed 291 permanently in 1917. Dove contented himself with showing in the Independents for that year, and exhibited a single blue and brown pastel in a Younger Painters Exhibition at the Pennsylvania Academy in Philadelphia in 1921. This little pastel (Dove later identified it as one painted from a Korean statuette) was occasion for Paul Rosenfeld to write in the December *Dial*:

> Even greater of avoirdupois, if as yet far less lubricated than that of Marin, is the virile and profound talent of Arthur Dove. And Dove, too, together with his great delicacy and tenderness, exhibits a grasp of the whole of life, takes in the animal with the spiritual, the gross teeming earth with a translucent sky. A tremendous muscular tension is revealed in the man's pastels. Great rhythmic forms suffuse the canvases; are one and swelled out to the borders; knock against the frames for egress. A male vitality is being released. One stands always, with Dove, one's feet "tenoned and mortised" in the ground. . . . And in everything he does there is the nether trunk, the gross and vital organs, the human being as the indelicate processes of nature have shaped him.

Dove's province was to be the earth, as Marin's was to be the sky. "It is easily within his power to give us the pageant of the soil, and do Whitman-work in Whitman fashion indeed."

Rosenfeld's appreciative writing grew into a volume, *The Port of New York: Essays on Fourteen American Moderns*, and again he refers to this particular

> brown and blue pastel of Dove's; and there is not a pastel or drawing or painting of Dove's that does not communicate some love and direct sensuous feeling for the earth. There is not one that does not bring us with a queer thrill close to some of the gross and earthy substances from which we moderns involuntarily shrink; and lay our hands gently on hairy animal hides, and rub them over rough stubbly ground, and pass good gritty soil through our fingers. They bring to the nostril the healthy pungence of pastures and barn-lofts. We are no longer afraid; *that* has been overcome; we rejoice in the warm udders of the cows; laugh at the grace of the young calf close to us; rub the palm over old pieces of used wood and palp their rough sides. . . . Dove begins a sort of "Leaves of Grass" through pigment.
>
> When this man paints, the pressure on the brush in his hand carries the weight of the body as a whole, and the life of the body as a whole. . . .
>
> For Dove is very directly the man in painting, precisely as Georgia O'Keeffe is the female; neither type has been known in quite this degree of purity before.

FIELDS OF GRAIN AS SEEN FROM TRAIN, 1931
Albright Art Gallery, Buffalo

The epoch was one of adventure in language also, of advanced Whitman-work: Joyce was writing, as were Sherwood Anderson and D. H. Lawrence. This Freudian rumpus of the barker before the tent must be taken in context, for in those days art *was* a sideshow and the public did *not* rush in. The prerequisite for the life of talent is a lack of embarrassment.

Dove had changed little in the past decade. His experiments had established themselves. AWALK POPLARS (1920) is all contrast and pattern for the artist; for the man in the woods all is tree, and for the squirrel the tree is a path: but it is the artist who wins. THUNDERSTORM (1921) is a perennial theme, the stylized force of nature, not unrelated to American Indian art in appearance and in intent. CHINESE MUSIC (1923) uses the familiar pronged shapes and saw-tooth forms. All three paintings grow directly out of THE TEN COMMANDMENTS—the development is in assurance, in performance.

But with STORM CLOUDS AND SILVER and MOON AND SEA, both of 1923, a change makes itself felt, a change in power and scope, as though the artist were aware of a larger world. Sun, moon, and sea will serve from now on as great omnipresent symbols, drawing Dove hypnotically. The earth painter is not keeping to his assigned territory. This lift into the sky is no accident: it follows another break toward freedom.

GOAT, 1935
Alfred Stieglitz Coll.,
Metropolitan Museum of Art, New York

HUNTINGTON HARBOR,
1926
*Mr. and Mrs. James H. Beal,
Pittsburgh*

Sometime around 1920 Dove left his family and went to live on what is variously described as a scow or a houseboat in the Harlem River. Soon he had bought a yacht from his friend Bill Hart. The *Mona* was no scow but a forty-two-foot yawl, twelve-foot beam, that had been in the Bermuda race in her time. "Lots of work on boat, on family, and on work, so far this spring," Dove wrote Stieglitz in 1920. "Hope more work will come soon, and that I shall be more prolific. No hope for or from the family. Brother here the other day as ambassador from Mother to get me to come home to see her, and 'to smooth things over,' but with too coarse sandpaper. Family first, safety first, duty first, and spirit last."

"So many things nice or otherwise have happened," he wrote the next year, "that I have been trying to put them all into action. Consequently [I] have not written and have five or six drawings or paintings that are almost self-portraits, in spite of their having been done from outside things. They seem to [me] more real than anything yet. It is great to be at it again, feel more like a person than I have in years. Trying to develop an ego—purple or red I don't know which yet. Think that is what has been lacking. You will understand. At any rate it must be done in spite of everything."

Dove lived aboard the *Mona* for seven years. He cruised Long Island Sound, haunted Port Washington, Lloyd's Harbor, and in the winter tied up in Huntington Harbor at Halesite by the Ketewomoke Yacht Club. Life on the *Mona* was strenuous, meager, not conducive to steady production. The cabin was cramped, and the paintings that came out of it were small even for Dove. He made his own metal frames with a blow torch.

The second Mrs. Dove shared this life. Helen Torr was a painter in her own right. Dove's letters to Stieglitz (now signed Reds and Dove) speak at length of her painting for many years. The two painters lived in devoted isolation, and eventually it was her life to be his audience. A letter to Stieglitz, dated February 10, 1923, conveys something of their adventure.

Dear Stieglitz:

It is now 3:45 AM in the midst of a terrific gale and we are anchored in the middle of Manhasset Bay held by a ¾ inch line run through a shackle to a mooring. We have been fairly pounding the bottom out of the boat for 24 hours and just hoping that line will have the decency not to cut through. Sheets of rain drive across the cabin roof and we are taking turns at watch and nursing a light fire in our stove until morning on a small pail of charcoal. Life has seemed this way for the last month. So full of contrasts that even they become somewhat monotonous. We think we would like a little rest for a few days—by that I mean a chance to paint.

We left Thursday at 7 AM and by the time we were well out in the Hudson that storm which you may have read of overtook us and we could not make headway against it and the tide so went with it until we made in behind the lighthouse at Ft. Washington 172 St. Pounded there all day and night and rewired the engine to be sure there was no leakage. Needed full power to get around the Battery the next day. Well, we made it, but felt a trifle as though we were creeping through 42 St. on a kiddie car. This boat is no speed demon. The ferrys, tugboats, etc., were very considerate —hardly noticed our efforts to keep out of their way.

They make about 15 miles an hour so suppose our four didn't seem so important to them as it did to us.

The engine held until we were in the East River at Brooklyn Bridge. After two hours of being hurled against a canal boat in a slip where we tied, found the trouble in a water valve that had stuck and heated up the cylinders. Also climbed the mast, fixed loose rigging and a bob stay under the boat that had broken—we made time in Hellgate as the current runs at about 5 miles and things fairly flew by. We made the Sound and this bay just as things started up again. . . .

Have been trying to memorize this storm all day so that I can paint it. Storm green and storm grey. It has been too dark and nerve-strained to paint so did three illustrations this morning just to keep from cutting the rope through by thinking so hard about it.

Was afraid Reds might not be able to stand the rough seas. She has been a wonder. Really has done the work of a sailor. This unity of interests is marvelous, so we are very happy. . . .

Will probably stay here . . . until the weather is fit to go back. . . .

The storm seems to be letting up a little. I hope it will stay that way. . . .

Our very best to you both.

As ever
Dove

FERRY BOAT WRECK—OYSTER BAY, 1931
Gift of Mr. and Mrs. Roy R. Neuberger,
Whitney Museum of American Art, New York

Another letter to Stieglitz of October, 1923, touches in details that describe a way of life.

> We have about decided to take this month to paint in on Long Island Sound rather than try to get South for the winter. There might be more trouble with the engine. . . . The O'Keeffe painting looks better than ever, especially in the boat here by the light of our lantern. [An O'Keeffe was the only painting that Dove kept on view.] Reds is painting again after our strenuous summer, and I hope to get at it again after a few days.

Stieglitz, meanwhile, had been only temporarily quiescent, and he showed his life's work in photography at the Anderson Galleries in 1921, with still more photographs two years later. At the same galleries in 1922 he held an auction of paintings by his artists. Paintings not sold would be destroyed, said Stieglitz—it was a question of space; and Philip L. Goodwin rescued Dove's SAILS by purchase. Despite the threat, there were enough paintings on hand in 1924 for a retrospective, Beginnings and Landmarks of 291, which included early Doves.

In 1925 Stieglitz opened the Intimate Gallery, 291's successor, in Room 303 at the Anderson Galleries. The first exhibition, Seven Americans, was on an extensive scale. The catalogue listed "159 Paintings, Photographs, and Things Recent and Never Before Publicly Shown, by Arthur G. Dove, Marsden Hartley, John Marin, Charles Demuth, Paul Strand, Georgia O'Keeffe, Alfred Stieglitz." Dove showed no less than twenty-five paintings and produced a poem for the catalogue.

A WAY TO LOOK AT THINGS

We have not yet made shoes that fit like sand
Nor clothes that fit like water
Nor thoughts that fit like air,
There is much to be done—
Works of nature are abstract,
They do not lean on other things for meaning
The seagull is not like the sea
Nor the sun like the moon.
The sun draws water from the sea
The clouds are not like either one—
They do not keep one form forever.
That the mountainside looks like a face is accidental.

The "Things Recent" by Dove were collages. In the past two years Dove had produced a dozen constructions—collage is too restricting a term—made of almost anything at hand, the only intangible ingredient being his sense of humor. Stieglitz had shown Picabia, and his painters knew all about the Dada movement. But Dove's collages were obviously an instinctive development, an outlet for the higher levels of the subconscious which come to the surface as wit, fresh with all the condensation that art requires. Dove had a word for his special use of nature, or of natural things, "extraction" rather than "abstraction," and he seemed to be thinking in terms of these collages when he wrote in 1927, "I should like to take wind and water and sand as a motif and work with them."

Among the collage, the exhibition contained the PORTRAIT OF A. S. (1925) MIRROR ON CARDBOARD, WITH LENS, STEEL WOOL, CLOCK SPRING. The title for once told all, that Stieglitz (A. S.) looked with a magnifying eye, that he mirrored and reflected, ticked on time with the century, and had unruly hair of the vitality of steel wool, or pubic hair, to stay with Rosenfeld's whole man.

GRANDMOTHER (1925) WOOD PANEL WITH NEEDLEPOINT, BIBLE PAGE, PRESSED LEAVES was unfortunately quaint and has perhaps given a folksy account of Dove to too many people. Dove's endeavor to fuse form and natural source in the symbol did not always succeed. Occasionally he only provided a label. Yet there was a healthy element of mockery in the technique. He showed in this exhibition a life-size MISS WOOLWORTH who has since rusted out. She was made of "mask, stockings, gloves, all Woolworth store purchase," and the critic of the *Brooklyn Eagle* "wanted to laugh but did not dare." *The*

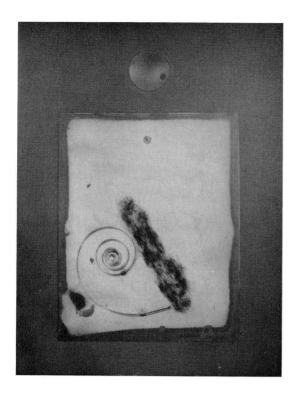

New Yorker told its readers: "You don't know what 10 A.M. March 24 interpretation of modern is until you have dwelt a while with Georgia O'Keeffe, Arthur Dove, and John Marin. . . . We are not liberated enough for the watchsprings . . . and other media that Arthur Dove utilizes for his compositions, but we can stand all day in awe before his storm clouds and abstractions." Derogation poured from the arch-conservative critic, Royal Cortissoz, now forgotten with his forgotten, and Heywood Broun defended Dove, bought his AFTER THE STORM, and soon began to paint himself.

RALPH DUSENBERRY (1924) OIL, CANVAS, WOOD is rich in the resources of the collage adventure, with its odds and ends put into evidence as a character study. In much the same fashion, the contemporary Scott Fitzgerald liked to build a personality with an inventory of habits, of things-found-in-the-pocket; Dove himself went on to explain:

> Apropos of the hymn in the "Ralph Dusenberry," the Dusenberrys lived on a boat near us in Lloyd's Harbor. He could dive like a Kingfish and swim like a fish. Was a sort of foreman on the Marshall Field Place. His father was a minister. He and his brother were architects in Port Washington. He drove in to Huntington in a sleigh one winter and stayed so long in a café there they had to bring a wagon to take him home. He came home to his boat one day with two bottles, making his wife so mad that she threw them overboard. He dived in right after them and came up with one in each hand. When tight he always sang "Shall we gather at the river."

51

Suzanne Mullett later offered an explanation which Dove endorsed: "A printed piece of the song is in the picture, the carpenter's rule as a symbol of architecture makes a frame; the flag, the patriotic nature of Dusenberry, and the arrow forms his diving and swimming ability; while the weather-worn wood shingles suggest water and sun-soaked piers."

But no sooner is the observer reconciled to a certain quaintness, or bizarreness of means, than Dove offers an unassailable creation, THE SEA NO. 1, (1925) ALUMINUM PANEL WITH GAUZE, SAND AND PAPER. He has scratched on aluminum a circle and a few radiating lines for a moon, covered it with gauze, and clamped the whole together between glass and frame; somehow the quality of moonlight is caught and placed in residence. There is something ineffable here. And yet these devices are too fragile, have too much of the maker's mortality in them, to have an independent life in art.

HUNTINGTON HARBOR (1926) OIL ON WOOD PANEL WITH SAND, CLOTH AND WOOD CHIPS exists in two versions for this year, No. 1 belonging to the Phillips Gallery, No. 2 to Mrs. James Beal. Both say that seeing is contact, that the eye feels shape, that shore things are gritty. The flatness of sails is here, the feel of how they hang and do their work, and in the Phillips Gallery example is the subtle mixture of the serenity and frustration of lying becalmed. GOIN' FISHIN' of the same year, made of sections of bamboo and old denim, is perhaps one of Dove's most characteristic, whimsical, and playful inventions. The collages, from 1924 to about 1930, form a complete and separate dimension. Their special quirk lies deep in their manufacture; no one has been more successful than Dove in creating genuine expression by these means.

RALPH DUSENBERRY, 1924
Alfred Stieglitz Coll.,
Metropolitan Museum of Art,
New York

THE BESSIE OF NEW YORK, 1932
Edward Joseph Gallagher III Memorial Coll., Baltimore Museum of Art

In the year 1925 Dove's father died. Ironically, the recognition that might have convinced his father lay immediately ahead. At Stieglitz's new gallery the opening, Seven Americans, was followed by a long series of one-man shows, first Marin over the end of the year, then Exhibition II, Arthur G. Dove, January 11–February 7. *The New Yorker* found that "the one-time painter of beautiful forms and now searcher after truth has gone to Plato for his defense, saying that first one must find truth, then go back and perfect the means by which he finds it. . . . He knows what he is doing, and is . . . entitled to follow his own star."

"The introspective cow, the derrick wheel, the storms, the sentimental music are all there." These are recurrent themes. The cow has been on the scene since 1911; the derrick wheel is either GEAR 1922 or a repeat. "The new things he has turned out this year are of the MISS WOOLWORTH variety," *The New Yorker* goes on. "Bits of driftwood, pine cones, sticks and stones, seashells, cork insulation, blue steel covered with chiffon"—the last almost certainly is THE SEA, No. 1. Edmund Wilson in the *New Republic* compared the collages to Rimsky-Korsakov's *Schéhérazade* played on the color organ, a "striking black and silver seascape over which inverted bowls of darkness descended."

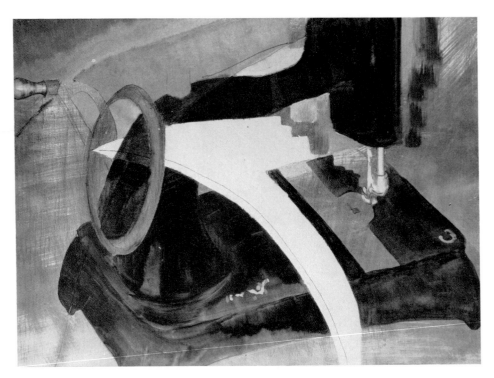

WATERFALL and GOLDEN STORM were purchased out of this exhibition by Duncan Phillips, and here began a lifelong interest. In GOLDEN STORM, Dove made use of swirling choreography. "With its overhanging clouds and . . . tremendous sense of movement," Phillips found it "a little masterpiece of vitalized pattern," as he wrote in his *Collection in the Making* published in 1926. This painting appeared in Eleven Americans, an exhibition held in that year at the Phillips Gallery.

The Société Anonyme included Dove in its International Exhibition of Modern Art in January, 1927, recognition that had to carry him over until the following winter; his next one-man show was Arthur G. Dove, Paintings at the Intimate Gallery, December 12, 1927–January 11, 1928. Of the nineteen items shown, the first six were given over to musical themes and a number were collages: I'LL BUILD A STAIRWAY TO PARADISE; GEORGE GERSHWIN'S "RHAPSODY IN BLUE" PART I, with PART II the other side of the record; ORANGE GROVE IN CALIFORNIA—IRVING BERLIN; RHYTHM RAG; IMPROVISATION. He had "become much interested in the melodies coming in over the radio. Experimenting with sounds he had worked out his own shorthand system that recorded sounds as music does on a scale—the musical scales were used vertically and the sounds were written by linear movements instead of notes."

GEORGE GERSHWIN'S "RHAPSODY IN BLUE" PART I, 1927
Downtown Gallery, New York

I'LL BUILD A STAIRWAY TO PARADISE and the first RHAPSODY IN BLUE, understandably two-dimensional and far removed from recognizable images, are as near as Dove comes to the language of Kandinsky. "The music things were done," said Dove, "to speed the line up to the pace at which we live today. . . . The line was a moving point reducing the moving volume to one dimension. From then on it is expressed in terms of color as music is in terms of sound."

Edwin Alden Jewell, critic of the *New York Times*, bought ORANGE GROVE IN CALIFORNIA and used it as the frontispiece for his book, *Americans*, published in 1930. Years later, in 1943, he defended his choice: "It belongs to a

RISING MOON, 1941
J. Vandenbergh Coll., Andover, Massachusetts

certain period . . . which I have always considered, in its way, Dove's 'top'! He has never to my knowledge done anything else like it—much more calligraphic than the paintings with their larger abstract forms that came afterward."

The larger abstract forms would be nobler, but Dove seems to have been easier at this period. He would never, perhaps, be as close to his public again.

In the next show, April 16–May 4, 1929, Dove had twenty-three canvases and no collages. Here was the handsome ALFIE'S DELIGHT (through misreading of longhand, sometimes called ALFIR'S), named for the pleasure Alfred Maurer took in the painting, a crescendo of circular expanding forms. Related to ALFIE'S DELIGHT in pattern though not in subject, FOG HORNS, also in this exhibition, is one of Dove's best. Images of the solemn hoot and blast swell out of their own caverns, as smoke rings out of cannons, the sounds rolling over the heavy waves, and an answering sound coming from the horizon.

For this exhibition Stieglitz published *Notes* by Arthur Dove. The notes appear after date lines, as fragments of a journal. These are the last two of five:

> Jan. 12—Just now I am trying to put a line around, in, and through an idea. After that, or at the same time, to thoroughly grasp or sense the light condition in which the idea exists. The rest is just trying to make everything you put down say the same thing in different ways as hard as possible, and with order, or disorder, if necessary, to make the sensation completely realized.

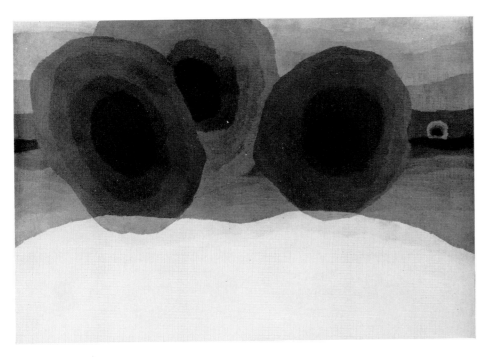

FOG HORNS, 1929
Oliver James Coll., Colorado Springs Fine Arts Center

ALFIE'S DELIGHT, 1929
Dr. & Mrs. Milton L. Kramer, New York

March 5—PERHAPS ART IS JUST TAKING OUT WHAT YOU DON'T LIKE AND PUTTING IN WHAT YOU DO.

THERE IS NO SUCH THING AS ABSTRACTION.

IT IS EXTRACTION, GRAVITATION TOWARD A CERTAIN DIRECTION, AND MINDING YOUR OWN BUSINESS.

IF THE EXTRACT BE CLEAR ENOUGH ITS VALUE WILL EXIST.

IT IS NEARER TO MUSIC, NOT THE MUSIC OF THE EARS, JUST THE MUSIC OF THE EYES.

IT SHOULD NECESSITATE NO EFFORT TO UNDERSTAND.

JUST TO LOOK, AND IF LOOKING GIVES VISION, ENJOYMENT SHOULD OCCUR AS THE EYES LOOK.

An excerpt from his unpublished notes assembled by Suzanne Mullett shows Dove's unsimple, simply stated approach:

How do you feel about a person when you're talking over the phone? If you know them, or if you don't know them, do you get something, do you put that into words of your own, from what they say, or from what you think? Or if it were music over the radio, have you ever tried to think how it would look?

If you have been asked to meet someone in another room whom you've never seen, it wouldn't be easy not to think what that person was like on the way into the other room. It would be surprising indeed if your idea of the person in the other room and the person in the other room collided precisely—they never could even if you had been in the other room all the time.

So what we know about objects is not so important as what we feel about them. So there we are being ourselves and we might as well do it. And point [paint?] and say what we feel in our own way.

Last night I told two men where to anchor. One . . . looking more or less like Sherwood Anderson.

They had a beautiful boat.

The Sherwood looking man asked me if I lived on the boat. I said, "Yes, all the year round for seven years, except last winter." The person whose name I knew not as yet said, "If you like the water that much, come across the Sound. I should like to have some one there. I have several cottages and two islands."

He said, "I am not in business. I'm a retired fool." A rather sad, strong, humorous person who is very fond of the sea. An human naturalist if that would be a description.

He described some rescues off the point there that were amazingly real. It is hard to give the simplicity of the telling. Diving for people who looked near underwater, but were too far away, then coming to the surface and diving again.

He insists upon coming for us either in his boat or car to move us into one of his houses for the winter, just to keep a light burning in his house so that the islands will look inhabited

Dove accepted and moved to Pratt's Island, Noroton, Connecticut, and spent no more winters aboard the *Mona*. The following spring he returned to Halesite. "Well, we are back here," he wrote Stieglitz in June, 1929. "It is much bigger country here on the whole and we are feeling more at home if that is possible. I wrote the secretary of this little yacht club here and offered them $5 a month for the top floor which is practically unused except for occasional dances. They called a meeting and gave us the top floor and use of the rest rent free just to have some one there. The room is full of light about 30′ × 40′. A bedroom off toilet lavatory, etc., gas and electricity and a wonderful view of the whole harbor. So our wish for a house on a dock where we could tie [up our] boat has come true. And we think it will work out for winter, too. Have been enclosing stairway doing floors, etc." Dove put in a stove, and he and his wife were overjoyed to be warm for a change. They lived in the Ketewomoke Yacht Club until March, 1933.

The annual exhibitions continued. Duncan Phillips was showing Dove's paintings in his Washington gallery through the autumn of 1930. The Museum of Modern Art, then newly founded ("suppose you have heard of the new Luxembourg," Dove wrote to Stieglitz in 1929), showed three of his canvases in its Painting and Sculpture by Living Americans, December 2, 1930–January 20, 1931.

Dove now produced such outstanding canvases as SNOW THAW (1929–1930), one of Phillips' early purchases. Then came SAND BARGE (1930), one of his finest works, with its bold flat color that submerges the out-of-the-window aspect and foreshadows his last great phase. SAND BARGE is advance notice of the painting that will dominate the coming quarter-century of American art.

SILVER TANKS AND MOON (1930) jostles Sheeler and Demuth at their architectural best, and DANCING TREE (1930–1931) has real gaiety and is one of the surest of the Dove ballets of natural forms. FERRY BOAT WRECK—OYSTER BAY (1931) is all prongs, spikes, and rust-reds of iron dying. THURSDAY (1931) has a sun-or-moon wedded to the water beneath, sky and water with no horizon divorcing them. Dove develops a texture here which he will use more and more; furred or feathered edges give an organic body to forms that can be precise without being metallic.

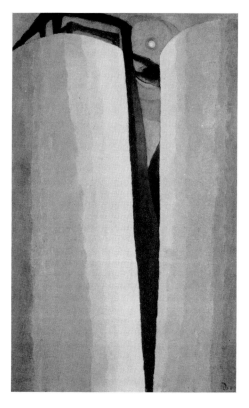

SILVER TANKS AND MOON, 1930
Alfred Stieglitz Coll., Philadelphia Museum of Art

60

COAL CARRIER, 1930
Phillips Gallery, Washington, D.C.

By 1932 a champion of Dove, Elizabeth McCausland, critic of the *Springfield Sunday Union and Republican,* was acclaiming his work. "The most abstract and theoretical of the Stieglitz group," she introduces him, "Dove has not perhaps had the succés d'estime of Marin and O'Keeffe." Comparing Dove's water colors and oils, "one may say that the sketches are freer and gayer; conversely the oils are stronger, more subtle, more suave, more abstract also of course. Both are masterly.

"Take the ferry boat wreck: its strong rotting timbers in the foreground set against the endless and incessant rhythm of the sea, pulsating in dull greens. There is a feeling of life, but also a feeling of art. . . ."

About this time Dove painted the vigorous BESSIE OF NEW YORK. The pilothouse windows of the *Bessie* are eyes. This personification is not Dove at his subtlest, but boats have long been symbolized in their figureheads or have had eyes painted on their bows, and no craft has a more emphatic and curmudgeonly personality than a tug. Dove always expresses a presence, whether it is epic, lyric, or just such a hunched muscular being as inhabits the *Bessie.*

From this period comes a record of a fragment of conversation held by Dove, his wife, and their close friend Alfie Maurer, who died shortly thereafter. They were discussing what constitutes American painting. The scene was the Doves' home in the Ketewomoke Yacht Club. The talk had turned on Klee and on Goethe's *Conversations with Eckermann*. Said Dove:

> When a man paints the El, a 1740 house or a miner's shack, he is likely to be called by his critics, American. These things may be in America, but it's what is in the artist that counts. What do we call "American" outside of painting? Inventiveness, restlessness, speed, change.
>
> Well, then a painter may put all these qualities in a still life or an abstraction, and be going more native than another who sits quietly copying a skyscraper. . . . People are bursting into print about their Americanism. . . . The American painter is supposed to paint as though he had never seen another painting. At least (they think) it would be desirable if he could.
>
> . . . The French go and come freely through the history of art, back and forth from the early stone cutters to their own hieroglyphic-like work everywhere along the road, taking what stimulates, adding, discarding, absorbing. How can one do otherwise? Even unconscious beauty is breathed in. Goethe said he knew some of his sources, but what all had gone to make up his intellectual maturity he couldn't honestly say. Aren't American critics being too conscious of "sources?"

CITY MOON, 1938
*Mr. Joseph R. Shapiro,
Oak Park, Illinois*

62

DANCING TREE, 1930
Mr. and Mrs. Donald Winston, Los Angeles

Dove was in the Whitney Museum's First Biennial Exhibition of American Art, November 22, 1932–January 5, 1933. Stieglitz showed Dove and his wife together in 1933: Arthur G. Dove, Helen Torr, New Paintings and Watercolors March 20–April 15, and in May, the Springfield Museum of Fine Arts showed Selected Early Works of O'Keeffe, Dove, and Marin. Elizabeth McCausland celebrated the occasion with a spread, "Water Color by Arthur G. Dove Presented at Museum," in which she gave a long forthright account of Dove's achievements. "Result, Dove lives on his houseboat on Long Island Shore, paints his pictures, grinds his own colors, makes his own frames, keeps himself and his wife (who had her first show this year at An American Place) on an income not as large as the welfare allowances many of the unemployed are receiving today."

The exhibition was in representation-held territory, and Miss McCausland cornered her New Englanders by telling them that "abstract art has never, however, been feared in the greatest cultures." Finally, she printed a letter from Dove which began self-consciously but went on to give one of the best and most mature accounts of his purposes:

> Description: On my driver's license it says: Date of birth, month 9, day 2, year 1880; color, white; sex, male: weight, 165 pounds; height, 5 feet 8 inches; color of eyes, blue gray; color of hair, blond gray.
>
> Have studied Latin, Greek, French, Spanish, some German and Italian; also farming, and how to make money. Succeeded with most of them and seem to have forgotten them all successfully with the interest that grew with painting.
>
> That has been the main interest to the point that all ideas become young and growing facts, and it is the growing of ideas into facts that is the sort of agriculture that interests me most. One so seldom gets a good breeder idea. Two or three in a lifetime would be enormous.
>
> That goes toward what is meant by modern painting.
>
> It is the human laboratory making research into life and all human thought and emotion to find young healthy plants that can stand the test of growing among things that are lasting through the ages.
>
> The making of objects that please the eye will always continue as will talent. The real breeder one is genius, the great sire. A great sire can make a whole section of the country fruitful and productive and the same is true of ideas.
>
> To save the finest and breed from it is better than saving all. That is what "modern" in the real sense means. . . .
>
> Just at present I have come to the conclusion that one must have a flexible form or formation that is governed by some definite rhythmic sense beyond mere geometrical repetition, to express and put in space an idea so that those with sensitive instruments can pick it up, and further that means of expression has to have grown long enough to establish itself as an automatic force.
>
> The play or spread or swing of space can only be felt through this kind of consciousness.
>
> To build a head and put on it hair and eyes and lips and ears like the handles on a jug is not enough. To make it breathe as does the rest of Nature it must have a basic rhythm.
>
> In other words, I should like to make a painting exist in itself.

From December 3 to the end of the year, the Springfield Museum displayed Selection of Watercolors by Arthur G. Dove, his first one-man museum showing, arranged by Elizabeth McCausland.

Before the spring of 1934, Dove's mother died. His family needed his help. He sold his boat, turned over a prodigious number of paintings to Stieglitz in March—twenty oils, forty-seven framed water colors, nineteen unframed—and moved back to Geneva.

THAT RED ONE, 1944
William H. Lane Foundation, Leominster, Massachusetts

Dove lived in Geneva for four years. They were difficult years, too difficult as it proved. The country was deep in the great depression, painting had lost its market, and the Federal Arts Project under Holger Cahill was rescuing artists as best it could. Dove, meanwhile, was far worse off than if he had never inherited property. He and his brother were land-poor. He struggled to bring order out of useless acres, confusion, and ill-timed development, only to face new liabilities and lawsuits as time went on.

He did not paint less. His annual exhibition presented its deadline regardless of his other involvements. He had reached his full maturity and was amazingly productive, all things considered. After three years his health, excellent until then, began to show the strain. First he had "heart trouble," then Bright's disease, a "gradual heart and kidney disintegration," as his son described it. His illness was very gradual, although progressive, and it was not clear to him that his predicament had gone into his marrow.

He missed Long Island and the sea. Almost at once he was writing: "Geneva weather, grindstone on your chest"; and soon after: "This is living in exile." An exhibition was coming up in April and May, and by March 30 he wrote Stieglitz of his struggle to get the work in hand.

> Your letter was even more thoughtful than ever. Understanding like that is almost unbelievable—that is if I hadn't known you.
> Another finished today.
> Have three more under way. I can send these and take measurements and send frames as I get them done. They could be put on the paintings and hung on some nails, if done in time.
> There will probably be about 15 new oils—hope to get them to you by the 10th.
> There are about 60 water colors, will frame what I can and send others in portfolio.
> Tenants have moved out of other house here so we move there next month unless it is taken for taxes. Upstairs here is like a boat cabin. Much more room there for work shop, etc.
> Hope you are in good shape. . . .
> Our love to you.
>
> > Always,
> > Dove

The next year the Doves left their little farmhouse and moved into the larger house "at the other end of the farm." They even made an effort to create a Dove environment with paint: "White ceiling, white doors, black surface, mars violet floors." His letters give progressive glimpses of his situation as he saw it. First he believed that he could set things to rights, then he realized that he must cut his losses. "[I] still think that there is plenty, and it must be the depression." But he admitted in the same letter, "[I] can walk a mile on our own land. It is just a waste."

Dove struggled to farm and to sell off land in small lots. He was involved in a lawsuit over a railway siding; he believed, apparently, that he owned at least the ties. His father had built a "Dove Block" in Geneva. The upper floor was an open hall used primarily for roller skating. It was a scene of winter activity, for he commented in February, "roller skating, prize fights, wrestling, and mobs at the Dove Hall. Now it [the attendance] is dropping, and ends in another month."

Among the earliest paintings from Geneva, DAWN II, like SNOW THAW, sets a dark in the very center of light, but now it seems a canker of evil in the center of good, an ominous theme that will be often repeated. DAWN III, a water color, is different altogether, an explosive work, showing objects that gain their blackness from the light as it catches them by surprise.

Now come two extraordinary paintings, A CROSS IN A TREE and MOON (1935), both images of witchcraft, both symbolizing the eye. A CROSS IN A TREE focuses on superimposed images held together by a rivet that is also a

MOON, 1935
Mr. and Mrs. Max M. Zurier, Los Angeles

pupil glaring down. MOON—Dove at his most evocative and intense—
catches the full moon in the top of a tree, but in a fashion to portray neither
moon nor branch, nor forest, only a single erectile torch that makes night a
territory of danger and joy.

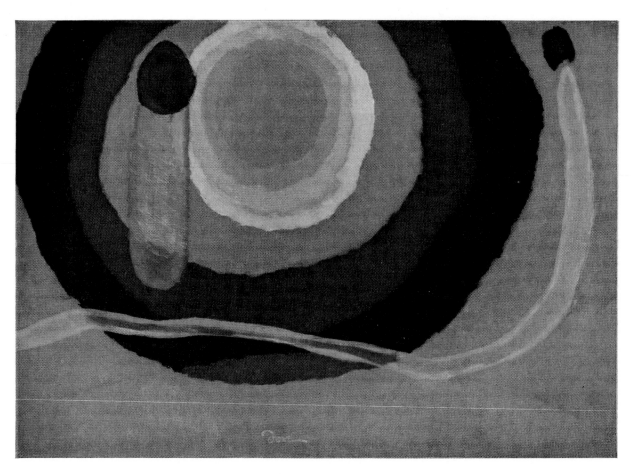

SUNRISE I, 1937
William H. Lane Foundation, Leominster, Massachusetts

Some inner solemnity was reaching for expression, and Dove paints suns and moons to which man has come too near, or which exert some Druidic power. RISE OF THE FULL MOON (1937) is relatively naturalistic, but the crack across the moon dial produces an ominous effect, as though all were not well overhead. The series, SUNRISE I, II, and II, all of this year, are almost a descriptive sequence in impregnation, if taken in such an organic sense: first the phallic intrusion, then the fusion as of a cell being reached, finally the same flaw or worm in the circle, which is life itself. But such a reading takes the paintings away from themselves; they are *not* precisely these things any more than they are precisely suns or the aurora borealis. First and foremost, they are events in paint.

68

SUNRISE II, 1937
Mr. and Mrs. Richard J. Gonzalez, Houston, Texas

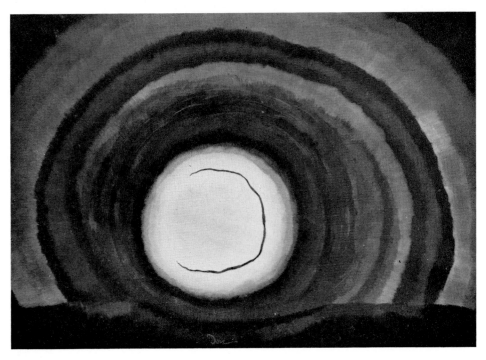

SUNRISE III, 1937
Kathryn Dreier Coll., Yale University Art Gallery, New Haven, Connecticut

The Geneva years were rich in water colors that were complete but not final, since they grew into oils. They constituted the original conceptions, even in scale, for many of them were postcard size. The paintings into which they solemnly grew were a mixed medium—tempera-based oils of a more formal, deliberate quality, in a technique that made much of flat, mat areas and restrained the sense of depth. "It is simply tempera (egg or casein) as an underpainting for oil color," wrote Phillips. "The ground is tempera on half-chalk ground." For other paintings Dove used tempera with a wax emulsion on a ground of talc and glue.

Late in this year, Dove wrote Stieglitz a subdued and moving letter about death—death coming to others but somehow nearer.

> That is a very beautiful thing that came today. Of course Marin is that kind of person.
> We had heard of Lachaise through a clipping Davidson sent.
> We did not know about Demuth. Reds and Clive knew him personally better than I did. Except through the work which I was glad to see, and I enjoyed his mental spirit so much as it held its hand up for Marin who writes so beautifully of that land.
> When people die I feel that they grow younger until they are born again. It must be something like that or nature could not breathe, as it does. It is not a sad thing to me as much as it is a part of a natural continuance. Of course I get lumps in my throat, but when I do, it is at the point of the realization of a fine truth. Alfy's case seemed to me to make the spiritual coming of age a trifle longer, but what has time to do with eternity?
> We are hoping to see Georgia in the next few days. . . .
> A whole painting this morning.
> Love to you.
> Please thank Marin for us.
>
> As always,
> Dove

Dove's mood gradually deepened. In CITY MOON the city, or window, is a barbed wire entanglement. HARDWARE STORE is not playful. The purposeful objects which the name calls up are entirely lacking. HARDWARE STORE is abstract expressionism in search of a name, and nothing could be more brooding and abstracted. But Dove had a way of finding a title in contemporary events as well as subjects—witness A NEIGHBORLY ATTEMPT AT MURDER. TANKS and POWER PLANT II are of man-made structures come alive, but not in Dove's former cheerful way. They are of a battered ruined materialism. The painter had none of the American respect for the builder; for Dove man-made things became grotesque when they were past their prime. Of the descriptive paintings, TANKS (1938) is one of the finest.

70

DAWN III, 1932
Mr. and Mrs. Sylvan Lang,
San Antonio

HARDWARE STORE, 1938
Mr. and Mrs. John Palmer Leeper, San Antonio

HOLBROOK'S BRIDGE, NORTHWEST, 1938
Mr. and Mrs. Roy R. Neuberger, New York

HOLBROOK'S BRIDGE, NORTHWEST is from the first half of this last year that Dove was still in Geneva. It is rich, solemn, and steeped in the connotations which the word or symbol "bridge" holds for painters, a passage from here to somewhere else, from now to the future. The covered bridge is an open vault, as grave-thoughts begin to stir and rise.

In February, 1938, Dove wrote: "Everyone in Geneva is dead or dying or just walking around. Guess we'd better get out.... We are trying to get moved for good. Can't keep up this moving and settling twice a year indefinitely.... [We will go to] Long Island, somewhere between Huntington and Port Jefferson."

He had sold the farmhouse for taxes the previous May. He and his wife moved into the Dove Block and took over the roller-skating rink, screening off such areas as they considered essential for housekeeping. The "only place unoccupied was this hall in the top of Dove Block. The block is mortgaged for so much that everything goes to the bank. So we thought we might as well use this to live in."

"We painted one wall white as high as we could reach, put a sofa and a couple of pieces of furniture in front of it, and hung up the few paintings," he told Suzanne Mullett. Their tumultous life in the skating rink was comparable to their life aboard the *Mona.*

A note to let you know that I'll be ready by the 20th if you need me.

Quite a swell wall of 24–5 paintings. My God. How they have gotten done I do not know. Fires . . . lawsuits. I really was worried about the work last Sunday. Yelled for Red to call the fire dep't. They were here in 2 minutes fortunately. Chopped a hole in the floor where I met O'K [Georgia O'Keeffe]. She will remember at head of stairs. A Western Union messenger boy had left a pail with a mop in it in basement on a gas plate—Just a bit more and we would have been gone. Warning among many others that we should get out of here.

Thursday we had to have a police sale of the Credit Bureau which I have wanted to get rid of for the last 3 years. Hope I do not get a lawsuit on my hands for doing it. But going cautiously as they are rather considerable crooks. A nice atmosphere for an artist. But sometimes the contrast is a help. It all takes so much time.

But—I have 25 paintings done and the frames almost done. Think I'll be ready to ship by 20th. That is a week before Marin is through. The things look big—different. I am not worrying about them. If they look big here they should there as this place is huge.

We want to come during the show and look around L.I. for a place for the summer or for good.

Another fire, fortunately they [firemen] only stop here occasionally. We are on the main square of the city so see and hear everything—even Salvation Army concerts every evening. Have listened all winter and are not saved yet.

General alarm just rang. Cop and district attorney on walk say "It must be a big one."

Reds is painting. . . .

Thanks for the Marins and check.

We'll be along soon after the paintings.

Much love to you all

Always,
Reds & Dove

It was not surprising that he pulled up stakes. He sent Stieglitz twenty-two oils, twenty-four water colors framed and forty-three unframed. He was back on Long Island in September.

LONG ISLAND, 1940
(water color)
*Mrs. Joseph Gersten,
Brockton, Massachusetts*

Dove returned to Halesite, and he soon found a place that suited him exactly. He bought an abandoned post office at Centerport, a one-room building about twenty feet square, backing on a tidal pond. The rear of the building stood on piers. Sea gulls flew by the window; swans maneuvered on the water. "We have one of those station stoves, and can spend the first warm winter in years." He was not well. Although it was September, "we have had to keep a small fire in a laundry stove." There was a "folding bed with black cover and elaborate head. All it needs is Cardinal Hayes."

The Doves were installed in time for the 1938 hurricane. "The trees all missed us but one that went through the roof. Water to our waists." The single room had a high ceiling, and after the flood he built in a new floor three feet higher, so that the window sills were at floor level. He is "learning to take it easy" now, as he continuously writes.

His mood was subdued, and he soon requited Stieglitz with his periodic word of gratitude. "Please know that I have never given a thought as to which [of the paintings] belonged to either of us. As I have often told you, they are as much yours as mine. And you have put just as much work and probably more thought into them."

Next spring he was "getting ready for that March 28 deadline" of the annual exhibition. Again he was not well: "Your letter *de Senectute* is the youngest and brightest thing I have had for some time." He had been "three weeks keeping his foot in the air. . . . It would be fine to be there, but the doctor is keeping me off my feet while working on the larger ones."

Dove was as cut off from New York in Centerport as in Geneva. By June 2, 1939, he was "still running temperature. Walked across yard for first time." But then, "the work is going fine. Am getting some new directions, as we think." And in August: "5:30 P.M., my present bedtime, but improving." He had a nurse, he got new glasses and was better, and then the nurse left. Stieglitz sent him a thousand dollars in October. Dove could not believe it. "They [the bank] are used to '100' and might imagine I had added an 'o.'"

Long Island, 1940 (oil)
Downtown Gallery, New York

He was incredibly productive. For his paintings he was no longer so dependent on the world outside. His canvases dealt with everything he had seen, as though a life were a day. Thunder Shower (1939–1940) shows the familiar prongs and the familiar crack across the center—the lightning flash; but it has also the quality of revelation, the instantaneous showing of vast forms which the flash illuminates. No Feather Pillow is a world of angered gods or surrounding forces that make no promise to remain in equilibrium. Such paintings are imbued with a great fatalism, yet they are so successful that they lift the viewer beyond the mortal circumstances that occasioned them. In January, 1940, comes the semidetached, courageous comment: "It is very gay here. A tractor has been sweeping the ice, and full-sized cars have been out here doing snap the whips. All the world on skates, and all the dogs on the ice. Quite amusing."

Month by month: The paintings "are improving so fast that the last ones do seem to be the best, which is not always the case. Have some large ones, 20 × 32."

"Going in to see Georgia's show."

"The Green Ball sold? I am bowled over, bumped off, or whatever one gets in times of surprise."

Long Island, in the midst of these months, is a painting of the whole natural history of an area. If it is geology, two glacier-deposited rocks sit in the brittle chop. If these objects are living things, they are blind creatures aware of each other, male and female, whalelike forms of whale size under a small distant cool sun.

By August he felt "in the best shape since first taken ill. He [the doctor] allows that I would not have had this last setback had a lady not tried to kill her two boys and succeeded with herself just outside here in the early morning. Having ears like an animal, it was a bit vivid for me." By the end of the year he reported that there was no evidence of a heart attack. The trouble was with his eyes, he hopefully reiterated.

The primordial forms he created in these summation canvases alternate with geometry, as in the simple interlocking rectangles of ROOFTOPS (1941), one of his uncompromising best, where the hanging together, the mystery in relationship, is managed through color. RISING MOON (1941) is a world of objects in their most generalized form: a moon is a great pod growing up into the sky out of a surf of color and a sea is broken by vertical teeth (of pilings?) that simulate vertebrae. Yet objects remain. ANONYMOUS (1942) is not a study in relationship, but of unknown things that must be related. For Dove, the idea is embedded in the object.

No painter followed instinct more confidently, and occasionally he was aware that his course was parallel to that of "primitive" art. INDIAN SUMMER (1942) is Indian, and SQUARE ON THE POND, of the same year, quite Navaho. PRIMITIVE MUSIC, dated two years later, frankly makes use of the lozenges, triangles, and rickracks that the Indians used to stake out the barren space around them, but this is only a development out of such examples as Dove's own THUNDERSTORM (1921).

Perhaps in our time, painters differ most in their choice of the moment of awareness in their own early history which serves them best. Currently the painter seems to locate himself in the moment when all is inchoate, whereas Dove always distinguished entities.

THE INN (1942) is a brilliantly self-conscious, yet sober environmental composite, a recast of man-made things; DEEP GREENS and MORNING GREEN of the same year are composites of another order where the separate colors stand for, or *are*, distinct species; they identify themselves as do the kinds of plants or trees in a jungle. In THE BROTHERS and PARABOLA of 1943, and in MARS YELLOW, RED AND GREEN, colors are the ultimates. Dove never yields to the totality of mysticism, an allover state of mind; he restates that the whole is made of elements inevitably separate in kind, as a red is separate from a blue.

The question then remains, if colors are absolutes, if *things* are so distinct, how, in what manner, are they to be related? Dove's answer is at once rudimentary and profound: *things* grow into complexity, and a work of art grows back into unity. His understanding that a painting *grows* makes him a modern painter.

Dove wrote to Suzanne Mullett in 1943: "A certain red, a certain blue, a certain yellow [and black] is the motif of one [of the sketches for THE BROTHERS] and brown, yellow, yellow green and black almost spells Mal-

THE INN, 1942
Mr. and Mrs. Milton Lowenthal, New York

lard Drake, under the window. Or raw sienna, black, and a willow green, the willow tree in front of me." *Colors* make *things.* "You can't get away from the color of a mouse."

In all this Dove defends the absolute existence of art. The anthropologist may set man against environment, or fuse one with the other, but there is something further which is not accounted for, hence a triangle, the "triad" of which Dove was so instinctively aware.

There seems to be a belief, among those who knew Dove, that his late trend toward abstraction was a function of his illness, of the extent to which his immobility cut him off from nature and threw him back on himself. Perhaps that is seeing a manifestation and missing the inner reality. Dove was not cut off; he threw away the extraneous, the unwanted. SAND AND SEA (1944) is more mysterious and compelling than the earlier sanded patterns; THE OTHER SIDE (1943) is language of form and color which cannot be lifted into consciousness and will not concern itself with any event.

The surface of existence, when he reverted to it, now took on a quality of transience. He was a man who looked up from his book in the days when only one man in a family could read: he put his magic aside to meet others on their ephemeral terms. He remained hopeful, clinging to the thought that his trouble was with his eyes. He had been to the dentist, he had new glasses, "large and bifocal." "Doctor put me in bed for a few days, but I am learning about how much can be done and how much not."

He wrote about an O'Keeffe show in Chicago, dwelt on wartime difficulties, on gas rationing. His doctor was called into the service, and the substitute doctor encouraged him. In January, 1943, a solitary sentence drifted in that equaled the paintings: "The sea gulls are flying by the window and their beaks look like ivory thrown slowly through space."

ACROSS THE ROAD, 1941
Mr. and Mrs. James S. Schramm,
Burlington, Iowa

78

Parabola, 1943
*Downtown Gallery,
New York*

If he saw too few people, he also saw too many, for he lived in one room. A refreshing whiff of the old battle with representation stirs him: "There are two or three that come here to fight. I asked him if he married his wife because she looked like someone else. He may have at that 'married his mother.'" By March of this winter he was still more cheered by the substitute doctor. "Old pump is best yet. [He said I] could stop taking digitalis."

More paintings flow around one central sun-moon focus: THE RISING TIDE, with its moon, the tidemaker afloat above its own commotion, and overlapping waves stirring both water and air, or HIGH NOON, a burning dark sun that has ceased to be a sun, become instead a color-absolute.

There are a few more diagrams in 1946, Dove's last year: FLAT SURFACES and BEYOND ABSTRACTION, in which he reiterates what he knows.
"I don't know what would have happened had we not such friends as you and Georgia [he wrote Stieglitz in June, 1945]. It is marvelous. I have been used to living in a world where if you didn't produce like a machine you were dropped like a hot potato. Now all these wonders have come to pass. . . . The stock of our great men is getting low now. So take good care of yourself."

Stieglitz was more than eighty, and he did not outlive Dove. There was a season of blankness, or unravelment, after Stieglitz's death. Georgia O'Keeffe had always concerned herself personally with Dove, had bought him early, and had hung his shows. But Stieglitz was not so much a dealer as an interpretive artist; with Stieglitz's fatigue and then disappearance,

ANONYMOUS, 1942
Alfred Stieglitz Coll., Metropolitan Museum of Art, New York

that composite which he and his painter had been, ceased to be. His painters had to be seen in a new context. Edith Gregor Halpert of the Downtown Gallery became dealer for Dove, O'Keeffe, and Marin. Edith Halpert, like Stieglitz before her, had dedicated her efforts to American art and to the recognition of the American artist; but approaches to art are as various as temperaments, and Dove now found himself shown to a wider public, learned that his work was wanted by a younger generation—people who knew nothing of his circumstances—and he felt the encouragement of cash in hand. He had a glimpse at least of his paintings going on without him into a life of their own. It was only a glimpse, but it at least told Dove what an artist most wants to know: he lives in his work. "I wish you could know how happy you made me feel," he was able to write, "that you are in charge of all the work and also we had a very fine day." Dove died in November, 1946.

At the end of Dove's life, large holdings in his work were in the collection that Duncan Phillips had built out of his choices from the annual shows, in the collection that Stieglitz left, and in the Dove estate. Georgia O'Keeffe gave from the paintings in the Stieglitz Collection to a number of museums, a fair beginning to the museum holdings that have grown since then. There has grown too, in the last few years, a new and large holding in the William H. Lane Collection, a collection of American paintings which Dove dominates. A determining factor, however, in the new, or revived, interest in Dove is Edith Halpert's belief in this painter's genius. Her's is a belief that has brushed away a view of Dove works as objects of a private taste; an assertive belief, based on a life spent working closely with the artists of our time. The Downtown Gallery's exhibitions of Dove have been numerous and significant, and have had a significant response in collections public and private.

The reaction to Dove's work since his death, with its inescapable irony, perhaps conveys something of the extent to which he was ahead of his time. He left behind a most curious discussion of the resistance to the new, written from Halesite in 1931, in a difficult period for him:

> When a few people all over the world have been fighting for an idea for years and bestowing all the care they can imagine on that idea, it would seem that it might by this time be understood, at least that the intention in direction might in the present civilization be known. If they refuse to read the writing on the wall, the part of art that is most alive will move on without them.
>
> There are many things next door that we do not see when we look so near.

No Feather Pillow, 1940
Munson-Williams-Proctor Institute, Utica

Light is always present, if we are not blind, and even the blind feel it whether they know it or not. The reaction is just different in different cases.

For those who try to weave the idea of comfort, by that I mean not endlessly trying to go beyond the last thing they have done for something further on;

For those who have no further wish than the expression of the things at the roadside:

For those who feel they must go back to the classic to realize themselves;

For all those who have given up hope of anything beyond;

For all those there is no hope.

It must be your own sieve through which you sift all these things and the residue is what is left of you.

They accept Bach, understand his idea and refuse Marin and Klee. I sometimes wonder whether these three are not grounded on the same love. One in his own realm of sound, one in his own sensation of space, and one in a colored measurement of life trying to combine the other two. They seem to be held just at the point where all the arts become identical.

It is the love of the sort of beauty that is above being so real that the fingers may be stuck in its side.

There could be no desire to change a perfect thing, no desire to chip off the edge to see how it was done.

One takes delight in leaving a perfect thing alone.

I sometimes wonder whether these violent antagonists can possibly understand the *Architectural Idea* that has gone to the making of the men they admire.

If these "modern" things are as bad as they think, there should be no real worry for them. If that were the case, the moderns would be the troubled ones.

When people find things "baffling," "defeating," "putting obstacles in their way," (and that is putting it mildly) they will usually find that they themselves are the obstacle, and their vocabulary becomes merely a stronger portrait of themselves, and I for one am amazed at some of these portraits.

HIGH NOON, 1944
Roland P. Murdock Coll., Wichita Art Museum

I know an old weather prophet who intensely dislikes the word barometer.

It should be time after all these years that the value of the new findings should be recognized.

People have more to do who are of to-day than those who are of the past.

Very few welcome ideas that are destructive to their own. If they are destroyed they naturally want to do the destroying themselves.

Enjoyment is easily distinguished from enthusiasm. Enthusiasm is flat and enjoyment is round, one is a projection of the other. And the heightening of all those feelings gives a hunger that is beyond the monument [moment?].

It is hard for a flat thing to understand a round one.

Once the earth was flat, but now it is round. Even yet there are a few who still insist.

Joyce is making a great attempt to feel completely round it, but almost free from audience.

Perhaps that is the way the world began—with no one looking on.

We go on doing what we do, earth and man and all, as in a ball.

THE RISING TIDE, 1944
Mrs. Ernest Frederick Eidlitz, New York

PAINTINGS IN PUBLIC COLLECTIONS

Addison Gallery of American Art, Andover, Massachusetts
Albright Art Gallery, Buffalo
American University, Washington, D.C.
Arizona State College, Tempe
Art Institute of Chicago
Baltimore Museum of Art
Brooklyn Museum, New York
Carnegie Institute, Pittsburgh
Colorado Springs Art Center
Columbus Gallery of Fine Arts
Cornell University, White Museum, Ithaca, New York
Des Moines Art Center
Detroit Institute of Arts
Encyclopædia Britannica, Chicago
Fisk University, Nashville
Honolulu Academy of Art
Inland Steel Corporation, Chicago
I.B.M. Corporation, New York
Lane Foundation, Leominster, Massachusetts
Memorial Art Gallery, Rochester
Metropolitan Museum, New York
Munson-Williams-Proctor Institute, Utica

Museum of Modern Art, New York
National Gallery of Art, Washington, D.C.
Norton Gallery, West Palm Beach, Florida
Philadelphia Museum of Art
Phillips Gallery, Washington, D.C.
Phoenix Fine Arts Association
Randolph-Macon Woman's College, Lynchburg, Virginia
San Francisco Museum of Art
Smith College Museum, Northampton, Massachusetts
Springfield Art Museum, Springfield, Massachusetts
University of Minnesota, Minneapolis
University of Nebraska, Lincoln
Wadsworth Atheneum, Hartford
Washington University, St. Louis
Wellesley College, Wellesley, Massachusetts
Whitney Museum of American Art, New York
Wichita Art Museum, Murdock Collection, Wichita, Kansas
Yale University Art Museum, New Haven, Connecticut

EXHIBITIONS AND CATALOGUES

(Exhibitions for which catalogues or documentation were available. See also Bibliography.)

1908 Paris, Autumn Salon.

1909 Paris, Autumn Salon.

1910 New York, The Gallery of the Photo-Secession.
    Younger American Painters. March 9–21.

1912 New York, Forum Exhibition.
  New York, The Gallery of the Photo-Secession.
    Arthur G. Dove First Exhibition Anywhere. February 27–March 12.
  Chicago, W. Scott Thurber Galleries.
    The Paintings of Arthur G. Dove: the paintings are examples of that new thought in modern art known as the Matisse Movement, Post Impressionism, or the more defining term of 'Expressionism.' March 14.

1914 New York, National Arts Club.
    Exhibition Contemporary Art. February 5–March 7.

1916 New York, Anderson Galleries.
    Forum Exhibition of Modern American Paintings. March 13–25, 1916. Catalogue.

1917 New York, Society of Independent Artists.
    1st Annual Exhibition. April 10–May 6. Catalogue. Two works.

1921 Philadelphia, Pennsylvania Academy of the Fine Arts.
    Exhibition of Paintings Showing the Later Tendencies in Art. April.

1922 New York, Anderson Galleries.
    Auction.

1924 New York, Anderson Galleries.
    Beginnings and Landmarks of 291.

1925 New York, The Intimate Gallery.
    Seven Americans. March 28.

1926 New York, Wildenstein Galleries.
    Exhibition Tri-National Art—French, British and American. January 26–February 15.
  New York, The Intimate Gallery.
    Exhibition II Arthur G. Dove. January 11–February 7.
  Washington, D.C., Phillips Memorial Gallery.
    Eleven Americans.
  New York, Brooklyn Museum.
    International Exhibition of Modern Art, assembled by Société Anonyme. November 19, 1926–January 1, 1927. Catalogue. Three works.

1927   New York, Anderson Galleries.
        International Exhibition of Modern Art, assembled by Société
        Anonyme. January 25–February 5.
        New York, The Intimate Gallery.
        Arthur G. Dove Paintings. December 12, 1927–January 11, 1927. Cata-
        logue, with note by Dove. Nineteen works.

1929   New York, Salon Américain.
        Spring Salon. April 16–May 4.
        New York, The Intimate Gallery.
        Dove Exhibition. April 9–April 28. Catalogue. Twenty-three works.

1930   New York, An American Place.
        Arthur G. Dove. March 22–April 22. Exhibition list. Twenty-six
        works.
        New York, An American Place.
        O'Keeffe, Demuth, Marin, Hartley, Dove (retrospective). April–May.

1930–1931 Washington, D.C., Phillips Memorial Gallery.
        First Exhibitions Season 1930–31. October 5, 1930–January 25, 1931.
        New York, Museum of Modern Art.
        Painting and Sculpture by Living Americans: Ninth Loan Exhibi-
        tion. December 2, 1930–January 20, 1931.

1931   Washington, D.C., Phillips Memorial Gallery.
        Second Exhibitions. February–June.
        New York, Grand Central Palace.
        Art Exhibition: Contribution of One Hundred American Artists to
        Voice the Need of Adequate Relief for the Unemployed. February
        25–March 5.
        New York, An American Place.
        Arthur G. Dove. March 9–April 4. Exhibition announcement.
        Twenty-seven works.
        New York, An American Place.
        Group Show (impromptu exhibition of selected paintings). Marin,
        Hartley, O'Keeffe, Dove, Demuth. May.
        Cleveland, Cleveland Museum of Art.
        Eleventh Annual Exhibition Contemporary American Oils. June
        12–July 12.

1931–1932 Philadelphia, The Pennsylvania Museum of Art.
        Exhibition. November 12, 1931–January 14, 1932.
        New York, White Plains, Westchester County Center.
        26 Paintings by 26 American Artists. December 21, 1931–January 16,
        1932.

1932   New York, An American Place.
        Arthur G. Dove New Paintings (1931–1932). March 14–April 9.
        New York, An American Place.
        Works by Arthur Dove, John Marin, Georgia O'Keeffe, Charles
        Demuth and Marsden Hartley. May 20–June 4.
        Cleveland, Cleveland Museum of Art.
        12th Annual Exhibition Contemporary American Oils. June 10–
        July 10.

1932–1933 New York, Whitney Museum of American Art.
　　　　　First Biennial Exhibition of Contemporary American Art. November
　　　　　22, 1932–January 5, 1933.
　　　　　Washington, D.C., American Federation of Arts.
　　　　　Abstraction in 1932. Season.
1933　　　New York, An American Place.
　　　　　Arthur G. Dove, Helen Torr, New Paintings and Watercolors. March
　　　　　20–April 15.
　　　　　New York, An American Place.
　　　　　Selected Early Works of O'Keeffe, Dove, and Marin. May.
　　　　　Springfield, Massachusetts, Springfield Museum of Fine Arts.
　　　　　Opening Exhibition. October 7–November 2.
　　　　　Springfield, Massachusetts, Springfield Museum of Fine Arts.
　　　　　Selection of Watercolors by Arthur G. Dove. December.
1934　　　New York, First Municipal Art Exhibition. February 28–March 31.
　　　　　New York, Contemporary New Art Circle.
　　　　　Paintings by Arthur Dove, Yasuo Kuniyoshi and Max Weber. March.
　　　　　New York, An American Place.
　　　　　Arthur G. Dove. April–May.
　　　　　Chicago, Art Institute of Chicago.
　　　　　A Century of Progress Exhibition of Paintings and Sculpture. June
　　　　　1–November 1.
1934–1935 New York, Whitney Museum of American Art.
　　　　　Second Biennial Exhibition of Contemporary American Painting.
　　　　　November 27, 1934–January 10, 1935.
1935　　　New York, Whitney Museum of American Art.
　　　　　Abstract Painting in America. February 12–March 22.
　　　　　New York, An American Place.
　　　　　April 21–May 22, 1935. Catalogue. Forty-five works.
　　　　　Cleveland, Cleveland Museum of Art.
　　　　　15th Annual Exhibition Contemporary American Oils. June 7–July 7.
1935–1936 Washington, D.C., American Federation of Arts.
　　　　　Travelling Exhibition. Season.
　　　　　Buffalo, Albright Art Gallery.
　　　　　Exhibition. December 25, 1935–February 6, 1936.
1936　　　New York, An American Place.
　　　　　New Paintings by Arthur G. Dove. April 20–May 20.
　　　　　Springfield, Massachusetts, George Walter Vincent Smith Art Museum.
　　　　　September 22–November 2.
1937　　　Minneapolis, Minnesota, University Gallery, University of Minnesota.
　　　　　Five Painters, 1937. Catalogue. Ten works.
　　　　　New York, An American Place.
　　　　　Arthur G. Dove: New Oils and Water Colors. March 23–April 16.
　　　　　Catalogue, with note by William Einstein. Twenty works.
　　　　　Washington, D.C., Phillips Memorial Gallery.
　　　　　Retrospective Exhibition of Works in Various Media by Arthur G.
　　　　　Dove. March 23–April 18. Thirty-three works.
　　　　　Cleveland, Cleveland Museum of Art.
　　　　　Exhibition of American Painting from 1860 until Today. June 23–
　　　　　October 4.

1938   Worcester, Massachusetts, Art Museum.
            Third Biennial Exhibition American Painting of Today. January 19–
                February 27.
        New York, An American Place.
            Arthur G. Dove. March 29–May 10. Twenty-eight works.
        Paris, Musée du Jeu de Paume.
            Trois Siècles d'Art Aux Etat-Unis. (Exposition organisée en collabo-
                ration avec Le Museum of Modern Art, N.Y.) May–July.
1939   New York, Museum of Modern Art.
            An Exhibition 10th Anniversary of the Museum.
        New York, An American Place.
            Arthur G. Dove Exhibition of Oils and Temperas. April 10–May 17.
                Thirty works.
        Boston, Museum of Fine Arts.
            Ten American Watercolor Painters. April 15–May 7.
1940   New York, Museum of Modern Art.
            Living American Art.
        San Francisco, Palace of Fine Arts, Golden Gate International Exhibi-
                tion; Art Section.
        New York, An American Place.
            Arthur G. Dove Exhibition of New Oils and Water Colors. March
                30–May 14. Catalogue, with note by Dove. Thirty-six works.
        Ithaca, New York, Cornell University.
            Spring Art Exhibition. May 19–June 3.
1940–1942 Washington, D.C., American Federation of Arts.
            Some Individuals. National Travelling Exhibition.
1941   New York, An American Place.
            Arthur G. Dove, New Paintings. March 27–May 17. Catalogue.
                Thirty works.
        Latin-American Travelling Exhibition.
            Contemporary North American Painting. May–December.
1942   New York, Museum of Modern Art.
            Cubist and Abstract Art; acquisitions and extended loans. March.
        New York, Museum of Modern Art.
            Painting and Sculpture in the Museum of Modern Art.
        New York, An American Place.
            Arthur G. Dove, Exhibition of Recent Paintings (1941–1942). April
                14–May 27. Catalogue, with poem by Dove. Twenty works.
1943   New York, An American Place.
            Arthur G. Dove, Paintings 1942–1943. February 11–March 17. Cata-
                logue. Twenty-two works.
        New York, Buchholz Gallery.
            A Backward Glance at Our Contemporaries. December.
1944   New York, An American Place.
            Arthur G. Dove—Paintings—1944. March 21–May 21. Catalogue.
                Twenty works.
        Philadelphia, Museum of Art.
            History of an American, Alfred Stieglitz: "291" and After. Selections
                from the Stieglitz Collection. Summer. Catalogue. Twenty-two
                works by Dove.

1945	New York, An American Place.
	Dove—Paintings 1922–1944. May 3–June 15. Exhibition list. Fifteen works.
1946	New York, An American Place.
	Dove—Recent Paintings. May 4–June 4.
1947	New York, Downtown Gallery.
	Retrospective Exhibition. January 7–25. Catalogue. Forty-one works.
	Studio City, California, Vanbark Studios.
	Dove Retrospective. February 7–March 15. Catalogue. Thirty-seven works.
	San Francisco, San Francisco Museum of Art.
	April 22–May 18. Fifty works.
	Washington, D.C., Phillips Gallery.
	June.
	Utica, New York. Munson-Williams-Proctor Institute.
	Dove Retrospective. December.
1949	New York, Downtown Gallery.
	Dove Watercolors. May 3–21. Announcement. Sixty-three works.
1951	Houston, Texas, Contemporary Arts Museum.
	Dove and Sheeler. January 7–23. Catalogue, with notes by Edith G. Halpert and Alfred H. Barr, Jr. Forty-one works.
1952	New York, Downtown Gallery.
	Retrospective. April 22–May 10. Catalogue. Twenty-five works.
1954	Minneapolis, Minnesota, Walker Art Center.
	January. Catalogue in Walker Art Center Calendar. Forty-three works.
	New York, Downtown Gallery.
	Dove Watercolor Retrospective–Dove and Demuth. April 6–May 1. Catalogue, with note by Alfred H. Barr, Jr., reprinted from Gallery's 1951 catalogue. Fifty-four works.
	Ithaca, New York, Andrew Dickson White Museum of Art, Cornell University.
	Arthur G. Dove 1880–1946: A Retrospective Exhibition. November. Catalogue. Fifty works.
1955	New York, Downtown Gallery.
	Collages: Dove. November 1–26. Catalogue. Eighteen works.
1956	Deerfield, Massachusetts, Hilson Gallery, Deerfield Academy.
	Dove and Sheeler, from the William H. Lane Foundation Collection. February 12–March 11.
	New York, Downtown Gallery.
	Special Exhibition of Paintings by Dove. (Paintings found in warehouse, 1946.) February 28–March 24. Twenty-two works.
	Los Angeles, Paul Kantor Gallery.
	Arthur Dove (courtesy Downtown Gallery). May 7–June 1. Catalogue, with notes by Alfred H. Barr, Jr., Robert Goldwater, from article in *Perspectives USA* (Number 2), and Frederick S. Wight. Twenty-five works.
1957	Worcester, Massachusetts. Worcester Art Museum.
	William H. Lane Foundation Exhibition here included a number of Dove's paintings. July–September.

SELECTED BIBLIOGRAPHY

BOOKS

Baur, John I. H. *New Art in America*. New York: New York Graphic Society, 1957.
———. *Revolutions and Tradition in Modern American Art*. Cambridge, Mass.: Harvard University Press, 1951.
Bulliet, G. J. *Apples and Madonnas*. New York: Covici Friede, 1930.
Cahill, Holger. *American Art Today*, ed. by Fred J. Ringel. New York: Library Guild, Harcourt, Brace & Co., Inc., 1932.
Cahill, Holger, and A. H. Barr, eds. *Art in America*. New York: Reynal & Hitchcock, 1934.
Cheney, Martha Chandler. *Modern Art in America*. New York: Whittlesey, 1939.
Cheney, Sheldon. *Expressionism in Art*. New York: Liveright, 1934; Tudor, 1939.
———. *A Primer of Modern Art*. New York: Liveright, 1924.
Eddy, Arthur Jerome. *Cubists, Post-Impressionists*. Chicago: A. C. McClurg & Company, two editions, 1913, 1919.
Eliot, Alexander. *Three Hundred Years of American Art*. New York: Time, Inc., 1957.
Frank, Waldo, Lewis Mumford, and Dorothy Norman, eds. *America and Alfred Stieglitz: A collection portrait*. New York: Doubleday, Doran & Co., Inc., 1934.
Jewell, Edward Alden. *Americans*. New York: Alfred A. Knopf, 1930.
Kootz, Samuel M. *Modern American Painters*. Norwood, Mass.: Brewer & Warren, Inc., 1930.
Larkin, Oliver W. *Art and Life in America*. New York: Rinehart & Company, 1949.
Mather, Frank J., Jr., Charles R. Morey, and William J. Henderson. *The American Spirit in Art*. New Haven: Yale University Press, 1927.
Mellquist, Jerome. *The Emergence of an American Art*. New York: Charles Scribner's Sons, 1942.
Neuhaus, Eugen. *History and Ideals of American Art*. Stanford, Calif.: Stanford University Press, 1931.
Phillips, Duncan. *The Artist Sees Differently*. Washington, D.C.: Phillips Memorial Gallery, E. Weyhe, 1931.
———. *A Collection in the Making*. Washington, D.C.: Phillips Memorial Gallery, E. Weyhe, 1926.
Poore, Henry Rankin. *Modern Art—Why, What and How?* New York: G. P. Putman's Sons, 1931.
Rosenfeld, Paul. *Port of New York*. New York: Harcourt, Brace & Co., Inc., 1924.
The World of Abstract Art. American Abstract artists. New York: George Wittenborn, Inc., 1957.
Wright, Williard Huntington. *Modern American Painting and Its Tendency*. New York: John Lane & Co., 1915.

MUSEUM PUBLICATIONS

Barr, A. H., ed. *Fantastic Art: Dada, Surrealism.* New York: Museum of Modern Art, 1936.

———, ed. *Masters of Modern Art.* New York: Museum of Modern Art, 1954.

———, ed. *Painting and Sculpture in the Museum of Modern Art.* New York: Museum of Modern Art, 1942.

———. *What Is Modern Painting?* New York: Museum of Modern Art, 1943.

Baur, John I. H. *Revolution and Tradition:* An Exhibition of the Chief Movements in American Painting from 1900 to the Present. Brooklyn: 1951.

Dreier, Katherine S. (text). *Modern Art.* New York: Société Anonyme for International Exhibition of Modern Art, 1926.

Eleven Americans. Washington, D.C.: Phillips Memorial Gallery, 1926.

Goldwater, Robert J. *Modern Art in Your Life.* New York: Museum of Modern Art, 1953.

Ritchie, Andrew C. *Abstract Painting and Sculpture in America.* New York: 1950.

Solomon, Alan R. *Arthur G. Dove 1880–1946: A Retrospective Exhibition.* Ithaca, New York: Arthur Dickson, Whitney Museum of Art (Cornell University Press), 1954.

Wight, Frederick S. *Milestones of American Painting in Our Century.* Boston: The Institute of Contemporary Art, 1949.

Yale University Art Gallery, *Collection of Société Anonyme.* New Haven: 1920.

ARTICLES

"Abstractions of Nature by Arthur G. Dove," *Art News* (April 10, 1937), p. 15.

"Age of Experiment," *Time* (February 13, 1956), p. 67.

"The Alchemist," *Time* (November 8, 1954), p. 64.

"The Art Galleries," *The New Yorker* (May 3, 1952), pp. 95–96.

"Arthur Dove," *Art News* (December 24, 1927), p. 26.

"Arthur Dove—An American Place," *Art News* (March 21, 1931).

"A Backward Glance at Our Contemporaries," *Art Digest* (December 1, 1943), p. 11.

Bennett, Rainey. "Arthur Dove—An American Place," *Parnassus* (April, 1932) p. 16.

Coates, Robert M. "The Art Galleries," *The New Yorker* (April 29, 1939), pp. 50–53.

———. "The Art Galleries," *The New Yorker* (May 18, 1940), p. 57.

———. "Exhibition American Place," *The New Yorker* (April 20, 1940), pp. 57–59.

———. "Exhibition at the Downtown Gallery," *The New Yorker* (March 10, 1956), pp. 120–121.

———. "Those Abstractionists Again," *The New Yorker* (April 8, 1944), pp. 62–63.

"Comment" and "Storm Clouds in Silver," *Dial* (August, 1925), p. 177.

Davidson, Martha. "Arthur Dove: The Fulfillment of a Long Career," *Art News* (May 7, 1938), p. 16.

"Demuth and Dove: Exhibition at the Downtown Gallery," *Art Digest* (April 15, 1954), p. 20.

Dove, Arthur G., *et al.* "Stieglitz," *Camera Work* (July, 1914).

"Dove's Form and Color," *American Art News* (March, 1912).

"Exhibition at An American Place," *Art Digest* (June, 1945), p. 14; (June, 1946), p. 14.

"Exhibition at An American Place," *Art News* (April 5, 1930), p. 12; (March 19, 1932), p. 9; (March 25, 1933), p. 5; (May 13, 1939), p. 15; (November 30, 1940), p. 11; (March 1, 1943), p. 23; (May 1, 1944), p. 19; (May 15, 1944), p. 7; (May 15, 1945), p. 7; (June, 1946), p. 50.

"Exhibition at An American Place," *The New Yorker* (May 2, 1936), pp. 59–60.

"Exhibition at Downtown Gallery," *American Artist* (March, 1947), p. 40.

"Exhibition at Downtown Gallery," *Art Digest* (January 15, 1947), p. 10; (May 15, 1949), p. 13; (May 1, 1952), p. 16.

"Exhibition at Downtown Gallery," *Art News* (January, 1947), p. 23; (May, 1949), p. 43; (May, 1952), p. 46.

"Exhibition at Downtown Gallery," *The New Yorker* (January 18, 1947), p. 22.

"Exhibition at Phillips Memorial Gallery, Washington, D.C.," *Right Angle* (June, 1947), p. 6.

"Exhibition at San Francisco Museum," *Architect and Engineer* (April, 1947), p. 6.

"Exhibition of Collages at the Downtown Gallery," *Art News* (November, 1955), p. 52.

"Exhibition of Collages at the Downtown Gallery," *Arts* (November, 1955), p. 50.

"Exhibitions of Paintings at the Downtown Gallery," *Arts* (March, 1956), p. 56.

Frank, Waldo. "The Art of Arthur Dove," *New Republic* (January 27, 1926), pp. 269–270.

Fulton, Deogh. "Cabbages and Kings," *International Studio* (May, 1925), pp. 144–147.

George, Laverne. "Arthur Dove," *Art Digest* (December 15, 1954), p. 11.

Goldwater, Robert. "Arthur Dove. A Pioneer of Abstract Expressionism in American Art," *Perspectives USA* (Number 2) (winter, 1953), pp. 78–88.

Gordon, J. "Flat Surfaces," *Brooklyn Museum Bulletin*, 17, 1 (1955), 27.

Haviland, Paul B. "Exhibition of Dove at Photo-Secession Gallery," *Camera Work* (1912), pp. 44–45.

Lane, James W. "Abstract Poet of Color at An American Place," *Art News* (May 15, 1942), p. 21.

McCausland, Elizabeth. "Dove, Man and Painter," *Parnassus* (December, 1937), pp. 3–6.

————. "Exhibition at An American Place," *Parnassus* (May, 1940), p. 43.

————. "Exhibition at An American Place," *Springfield Sunday Union and Republican* (April 22, 1934).

Mumford, Lewis. "The Art Galleries," *The New Yorker* (April 1, 1933), pp. 34–35; (May 5, 1934); (March 2, 1935), p. 38

"Newly Discovered Paintings at the Downtown Gallery," *Art News* (March, 1956), p. 50.

"Newly Discovered Work Shown at the Downtown Gallery," *Art in America* (spring, 1956), p. 57.

Obituary, *Art Digest* (December 1, 1946), p. 14.

Obituary, *Art News* (December, 1946), p. 9.

Pemberton, Murdock. "The Art Galleries," *The New Yorker* (March 21, 1931), pp. 64–66.

————. "The Art Galleries—For the Elect," *The New Yorker* (March 26, 1932), p. 34.

————. "At the Art Galleries," *The New Yorker* (March 28, 1925); (February 13, 1926); (December 24, 1927); (April 20, 1929); (April 5, 1930).

————. "Critique Art," *The New Yorker* (January 23, 1925).

Phillips, Duncan. "The Art of Arthur Dove," *New Directions Annual*, 11 (1949), 509–512.

———. "Original American Paintings of Today," *Formes* (January, 1932), p. 198.

"Phillips Museum Buys Four from Arthur Dove Show," *Art Digest* (May 15, 1935), p. 16.

"Retrospective Show of Watercolors at the Downtown Gallery," *Art News* (April, 1954), p. 43.

Riley, Maude. "Arthur Dove at An American Place," *Art Digest* (March 1, 1943), p. 9.

Rosenfeld, Paul. "American Painting," *Dial* (December, 1921), pp. 665–666.

———. "Art—After the O'Keeffe Show," *The Nation* (April 8, 1931), pp. 388–389.

———. "Dove and the Independents," *The Nation* (April 27, 1940), p. 549.

———. "Dove's Work in Comparison with European Moderns," *Dial* (June, 1925).

———. "Musical Chronical," *Dial* (June, 1925), pp. 530–531.

———. "The World of Arthur G. Dove," *Creative Art* (June, 1932), pp. 426–430.

Seligmann, Herbert J. "Why Modern Art," *Vogue* (October 15, 1923).

"Semi-Abstract Landscapes at An American Place," *Art News* (April 13, 1940), p. 13.

Shelby, Melvin Geer. "Around the Galleries," *Creative Art* (May, 1932), p. 395.

Soby, James T. "Arthur Dove and Morris Graves," *Saturday Review of Literature* (April 7, 1956), pp. 32–33.

Wilson, Edmund. "Opera Comique," *New Republic* (January 20, 1926).

PAINTINGS REPRODUCED